LIFE
TO
THE FULL

LIFE
TO
THE FULL

REFLECTIONS ON THE SEARCH
FOR CHRISTIAN FULFILLMENT

by John Heagle

THE THOMAS MORE PRESS
Chicago, Illinois

ISBN 0-88347-063-2

ACKNOWLEDGMENTS

The author wishes to thank the following for permission to quote copyrighted material from their publications.

Excerpts from *The Jerusalem Bible*, copyright 1966 by Darton, Longman & Todd, Ltd. and Doubleday and Company, Inc. Used by permission of the publisher.

Lines from *Selected Works*, Vol. I, Poetry by Stephen Vincent Benét. Used by permission of Farrar and Rinehart, Inc., 1942.

Lines from the *Poems and Prose of Gerard Manley Hopkins*, by Gerard Manley Hopkins. Used by permission of Penguin Books Edition, 1968.

Excerpt from *Rabbit, Run* by John Updike. Fawcett World Library Edition, 1969. Used by permission of the publisher.

Excerpt from *An Autobiography, The Story of My Experiments With Truth*, by M. K. Gandhi. Beacon Press, 1969. Used by permission of the publisher.

For Paula

CONTENTS

Chapter One

How Can We Know the Way?

THE SEARCH FOR A DIRECTION

The trail turned sharply at the edge of a small clearing and then moved into thick woods. I walked on with growing urgency. Without my noticing, it had become dark. We had been on the trail all day. When we stopped to make camp, I set out in search of water. I had no idea how much further I had walked. The map indicated a spring nearby, but I found no sign of it. I was aware of anxiety growing within me. At first, it was only a vague insecurity tinged with weariness. Then, in a wave of panic, it became clear: I didn't know the way back. I was lost. I searched the darkness for a familiar landmark but the underbrush all looked alike. I looked for signs along the trail but I recognized nothing. The woods had become a tangle of shadows. The trail was only a dark opening through the underbrush. I had lost all sense of direction.

For a few minutes, my pace quickened even more. My heart was beating wildly from exertion and fear. Finally, exhausted, I stopped. I forced

9

myself to stand still. In the darkness, I listened to the sounds of the night. I tried to calm my fears enough to think. Then, whether from desperation or from a long remembered intuition, I was looking up into the night sky. Long ago, my grandfather had taught me how to locate the North Star. It came to me now with an experienced instinct born of many quiet walks at night: Find the Big Dipper, then count five lengths from the pointing star—that's Polaris. Through the tree branches, almost directly above and in front of me, in the same direction that I had been walking, I saw the outlines of the Big Dipper, upside down as it is in early Spring. There, slightly to the right, was the North Star.

A sense of calm moved through me. I had discovered a still point. The world was anchored somewhere. The polar point in the sky reflected itself inside me. I felt in touch with my center, as though there were a still point inside of me also. The woods were as dark and unfamiliar as ever, but I saw them in a new way. I knew that the camp was behind me. I needed only to turn around and walk back.

My experience in the woods was a passing event that took place several years ago, but I reflect on it often. It remains with me not only as a memory but as a reference point. It provides me with a way of understanding the struggle that unfolds beneath the surface of my life and the lives of many others.

There is a common feeling that moves like an undertow through the lives of many Christians today. I hear it spoken of in different ways. It is not a feeling that can easily be described because it is so immediate and personal. The signs of its presence are varied and often contradictory. But those who experience it share one thing in common: They have a feeling of being *lost*. In our time, the Christian life has become a night pilgrimage. An inward sense of direction has disappeared. The way is still there, but the familiar landmarks are gone. The trail signs are confused or not recognizable. Sometimes, the trail is not visible and there is only the underbrush and the woods. A night of doubt has descended.

For some it is a feeling of dissatisfaction with the Church and with their lives. They speak of feeling let down or left out. For others it is a growing sense of insecurity. They speak of a lack of continuity with the past. They are bewildered without knowing why.

Many try to explain this feeling of uneasiness as a natural phenomenon that manifests itself during any time of change and upheaval. They point to the new forms of worship, to the changes in the structures and the shifting roles within the community of faith as the reason for their feeling of disorientation. They point to the explosive change that is taking place in society, in life styles, and in the forms and uses of technology.

All of these forms of change have contributed to the feeling of being lost, but they do not explain or touch its true depth. Change and upheaval may be the occasion of the feeling, but the experience itself is related to something deeper in our lives.

Those who are struggling to find a direction know instinctively that more is at stake than a debate regarding structural changes in the Church. Many Christians have become so discouraged that they have given up along the way. Others have wandered off in different directions, aimlessly or deliberately. But the majority are still walking, still searching, still struggling, still afraid. Most of these are people who were born into the faith and raised in a context of order and stability. They often find themselves looking back and wondering what has happened. Christian life was no easier in the past. But the demands were clearer, the way was more distinctly marked out, the directions were many and specific. When one observed the guideposts and followed the directions, there was a sense of fulfillment and satisfaction. There were ways of measuring personal progress and criteria for success or failure. Now the terrain is unfamiliar. The markers are gone, and it is night. In the last decade, we could point to change as the cause of our confusion. We now realize that it

is more than a question of change. The struggle to
find a direction is more radical than the attempt to
come to grips with new forms of worship or ritual. It
is beyond what we once thought were the burning
issues of theological debate: celibacy, birth control,
and authority structures. The feeling of being lost is
nothing less than a crisis of *faith*. It is *belief* itself
which is at stake in our time.

At times of transition, we find ourselves driven
back to essentials. I have learned painfully over the
last years that we cannot take faith for granted. It is
a gift, but it is not a given. It must sometimes be
received in the night with searching eyes and a new
heart. It is, in the end, a matter of believing. We are
engaged in what Kierkegaard calls the leap of faith.

Those of us who were born and raised as Christians are embarrassed that we are having doubts.
We feel awkward and even guilty because we have
lost our way. But the questions persist and we must
face them. Do I still believe in the Christian gospel?
Can I believe in *anything?* Is there meaning in the
Christian vision? Why pray? Does it make any difference? How do I know what is right and wrong for
me? Who will tell me? Where can I find fulfillment?

These are questions of pilgrims in search of a still
point. These are the honest cries of wrestlers of the
spirit who, like Jacob, struggle in the night with
themselves, with their world, and with their God.

Perhaps the true *aggiornamento* is only beginning—
the inner renewal of the life of faith in each of us.
We are searching together for a sense of direction,
for a new way of seeing. We seek for a still point in
the night. We look for the polar experience of faith.

The feeling of being unsure about our faith is an
unsettling experience. We have not yet grown
accustomed to standing on the edge of crisis or of
living, as Hemingway says, in the "eye of the
storm." But there is a creative side to the experience of losing our way. It challenges us to look in
new ways and in new places. It summons us to stop
for a moment, to listen to the silence, to embrace
even the insecurity and the fear. It invites us to take
time for reflection. In the struggle to relocate the
personal roots of our faith, we rediscover the experience of being pilgrims. Only those who set out
on a journey risk being lost. Only those who search
for life will know the anguish that leads to new
vision. The struggle to believe can be as growthful
as it is demanding.

The feeling of being lost is neither new nor un-
usual. It goes back to our roots. The search for faith
puts us in touch with the history of our religious
tradition—with all those who seek for the God of
Abraham, Isaac, and Jacob. And for the God of
Jesus, who we dare to call *our* Father.

Abraham is remembered as the father of believers. Yet, his life is the story of a struggle to believe and to continue to trust in Yahweh when all the landmarks were gone. It was the leap of faith which first enabled Abraham to respond to the call. He left behind his country, his culture, his people, and his land to follow the living God on a journey whose destination remained unknown to him. Abraham set forth with confidence. But it is one thing to set out on the pilgrimage of faith. It is another to remain faithful to the journey when the promises do not appear to come true or when one loses the way.

After years of wandering, Abraham had grown old, too old to have children. And he and Sarah had no children. He continued to roam the deserts with his flocks. He knew all the grazing places and the water holes. But in the wilderness of faith, he was lost. Inside, there were questions and unspoken doubts. What about God's promises? Were they only delusions and restless nightmares? What about the future? What did it all mean? Abraham's faith was put to the test when he realized that, humanly speaking, his future had no promise. Everything depended upon God. In a moving scene, the Book of Genesis describes Abraham in his tent, old and discouraged, a nomad without direction, a believer struggling with belief, a desert traveler lost along the way. Then God spoke to Abraham and invited him to come outside his tent. "Look up to heaven and count the stars, if you can. Such will be your descendants" (Gn 15:5). Abraham looked up and, in looking up, he found his way. He discovered the presence of God's fidelity enveloping him, holding him in love. Once again, he made the leap. "Abraham put his faith in Yahweh who counted this as making him justified" (Gn 15:6).

In the night there is the still point of faith. Abraham found that still point only by walking through the doubt and uncertainty, through the "terrifying darkness" which enveloped him (Gn 15: 12). Abraham is remembered as the Father of all believers, not because believing came easy for him but because he found a way of looking up. In the night, he still looked for stars. In the vast reaches of his own heart, he discovered the still point that is the living God.

The feeling of being lost did not end with Abraham. His descendants also lost their way. The Israelites remembered the mighty hand of Yahweh and his power which freed them from Egypt and set them on a journey toward a new land. But they also remembered the desert. They recalled the experience of being lost, the grumbling voices, and the backward glances toward the secure days in Egypt. They remembered the hungry faces, the discouragement, and the confusion. "You have brought us out here to die" they said to Moses (cf. Ex. 16:3).

They remembered the experiences of doubting, of wondering, and of wrestling with despair. They knew what it meant to walk without a direction.

Yet, it is the desert search which becomes Israel's most cherished memory. The prophets refer to it as the time when Israel was closest to Yahweh. The desert journey becomes the symbol of their intimacy with God, a time of purification and struggle, but also a time of breakthrough to convenant and community. In the desert, Yahweh led his people with a cloud by day and a pillar of fire by night. For the Israelites, as for Abraham, faith was the willingness to scan the skies, to look at the stars, and to keep on walking. Faith is a direction one finds in the wilderness. It is the vision that comes as a gift when we look in a new place.

The patriarchs of the new Israel are the apostles, those chosen by Jesus to be his companions and his friends. We are so accustomed to seeing the apostles as statues that we forget that they were fishermen and tax collectors, political radicals and searchers. Like Abraham, like the desert people before them, like us, they are pilgrims.

The new people of God began with a small community of those who felt lost. The scene is the upper room. Jesus knows with fearful certainty that it is his last meal with his friends. He washes their feet. He breaks bread and passes the cup. He shares his

heart with them. He speaks of love and service, of
fidelity and joy. When he speaks of going away, he
reads the fear in his friends' eyes. Jesus wants to
reassure them. He speaks to them of trust and of
journey. "Do not let your hearts be troubled. Trust
in God still and trust in Me. There are many rooms
in My Father's house; if there were not, I should
have told you. I am going now to prepare a place for
you, and after I have gone and prepared you a place,
I shall return to take you with me; so that where I
am, you may be too. You know the way to the place
where I am going" (Jn 14:1-4).

Thomas, the doubter, the spokesman for all those
who lose their way, asks Jesus: "Lord, we do not
know where you are going, so how can we know the
way" (Jn 14:5)?

Thomas speaks for every person who walks into
the dark night of faith. He and the other disciples
have been with Jesus for a long time. They thought
they understood what he had been saying and doing.
But now the darkness comes. The gospel describes
it in simple, direct words: "Night had fallen" (Jn
13:330). Thomas and the other disciples seek des-
perately for a still point in the midst of their confusion. They are struggling with faith. We are told
in the scriptures that the name Thomas means twin.
Nowhere does it say whether Thomas actually had a
twin. Perhaps what is implied is that we are all

Thomas' twins, for, like him, we, too, are doubters. We, too, do not know the way.

Where are you going? How can we know the way? Jesus' response to Thomas reveals the personal nature of faith. He does not give Thomas a set of rules or religious guidelines. He does not speak of the way as though it were merely a teaching or an intellectual exercise that leads to enlightenment. Instead, Jesus invites Thomas to enter into a relationship of trust and love. "I am the Way, the Truth, and the Life. No one can come to the Father except through me. If you know me, you know my Father too. From this moment, you know him and have seen him" (Jn 14:6-7).

Jesus is the still point of faith. He is the pathway to life and growth. Jesus is the polar experience that gives direction and meaning to our lives. He invites his disciples to look up, to look into his eyes, and to see there the light of the world. Christian faith is centered in a relationship of trust with the risen Christ. It is a new way of seeing. It is a vision not of intellectual understanding, but of shared love. Faith enables us to look into the eyes of other persons and to discover there the presence of the Lord who still pitches his tent with his people.

In these meditations, I want to explore the contemporary Christian's search for fulfillment. I have deliberately chosen to begin with the struggle to believe. Faith is the pearl of great price. Without faith the world is a field without treasure, a wilderness without direction. To speak of fulfillment from the perspective of Christianity is to explore an experience and a pilgrimage which is far different, perhaps even contradictory, when compared to the usual pursuit of human satisfaction. "Without a vision, the people perish," writes the author of Proverbs. Without the vision of faith and the still point which it provides, Christian fulfillment appears to be contradictory and even absurd.

The contemporary search for fulfillment often begins with the assumption that fulfillment is something we do for ourselves, an end in itself. Seeing is believing, we say. I want my piece of the action—all the good things of life that will meet my needs and fulfill my dreams. This attitude has made the quest for self-fulfillment a preoccupation of our age. It has become the barometer of success and the test of happiness.

The Christian search for fulfillment begins from a different standpoint. It begins with the leap of faith. It assumes nothing. It risks everything. Christians begin the journey of faith by trusting the darkness around them. They trust that *believing is a way of seeing.* Christians often feel lost today because they feel out of step with the current consensus on what constitutes the "good life." There is very little room for the cross in the contemporary pursuit of fulfillment. There is small space for suffering in a world which pursues fulfillment as an end in itself. There is no time to die, no room for pain. As a result, there is little room for resurrection or for the heart-expanding joy that Jesus promises those who follow him.

The Christian search for fulfillment begins with the crisis and the question of faith. It calls us to a new creation based on the paradox of the gospel, the foolishness of the cross, and the promise of resurrection. The struggle to believe is the most important inward event of our age. If Christianity offers any claim to human fulfillment, it must emerge from this wrestling of the spirit.

These meditations are invitations to stop and catch our breath, to reflect on where we are, and to accept, if necessary, the experience of being lost. They are intended to be a quiet call to prayer, a summons to explore the inner space of our lives, and to scan the skies of the self for a still point.

To develop the analogy further, we can say that the North Star is Christ himself, the light of the world, the still point of all creation. Faith is the centering experience of our human life. It is like the Big Dipper. It provides us with a way of seeing that leads to an encounter with God. Just as the Big Dipper assumes many different positions in the changing seasons of the sky, so our faith has taken many different forms and cultural expressions in the history of the Church. But whatever form faith assumes, it always centers our vision on God. It points to the polar experience of all life. Without faith, the night is ablaze with myriads of stars, but all of them are silent, all of them cold. Without faith, there is no center, no direction.

The faith struggle is carried on only in the context of prayer. There is the temptation to keep on running or to allow our panic to blind us to our need for reflection. We live constantly with the urge to run on ahead blindly, to keep busy, to engage in feverish activity, to take flight into the darkness, or simply to give up. Prayer is ultimately a stance of receptivity and discovery. It is most powerfully experienced at those moments when we have the courage to stop running and to allow the night to make us still. To meditate is to stop along the way, to embrace the silence, and to find our own center.

Chapter Two

Like the Deer that Yearns

THE HUNGER FOR FULFILLMENT

The river was less than a mile from where we lived. After we had finished the haying or at the end of the threshing season my brothers and I would walk down the dirt road with our fishing poles. First, we went swimming. The water was warm and lazy. It washed over us like summer. Later we wandered off by ourselves to fish. Usually, I waded downstream where the rapids rose. There the river curved gently, its banks lined with elm and maple. Standing in the rapids, I could watch the sun glisten on the water and the river disappear into the blue hills to the south. I seldom got a strike. I didn't tell my brothers then, but I went to the rapids more for the view than for the fishing. I went there to discover the flow of feelings that moved inside me like the river current. I was drawn to the solitude. I savored the silence.

But there was another feeling that brought me to that place in the river. Sometimes it was intense and deep. At other times it was only a quiet presence. Part of it was a restlessness, a reaching out like the river for the next bend or for the ocean. There was also a sense of aloneness—a coming home to the inner world where dreams are born. Standing in the current was like being part of the flow of life. The river seemed to flow through me, creating a feeling of expectancy, the stirring of possibility and promise. But the underlying feeling was one of longing, an indescribable sense of yearning. It was a longing without an object, a yearning without shape, a feeling without form. I had no words to give it expression. I can only describe it as a hunger of the heart for something beyond itself.

These moments of longing, these times of restlessness, are part of every person's experience. They are not visions from another world. They are simply the intensified awareness of *this* moment. They are occasions when the texture and flow of experience rise in us like rapids, glisten for a moment in the sunlight, and then disappear, leaving us with the gift of wonder.

The human heart is a hunger for life. This seeking quality of our inward self is revealed in the most ordinary circumstances. We might experience it when we are gazing absentmindedly out a window; when we hear a song on the car radio; when we look for a familiar face in a crowd of strangers; or when we return from a gathering of friends and feel a sudden wave of loneliness.

This longing comes into our lives at times of transition: When a mother notices that her little girl has become a young woman; when we leave home for the first time; when we stand in a train station and wave at a friend disappearing in the morning rain; when we pack up our belongings to move to a new city and a new job.

The experience of yearning can arise on occasions of great joy or sorrow: When a college graduate looks into his father's eyes, smiles broadly, and says: "Thanks, Dad"; when the phone rings in the night with news of a death in the family; when we sit helplessly at a bedside and search for a word to share with someone who has just been told that she has terminal cancer.

It comes as a vague restlessness: At night when we cannot sleep, or on vacation when we cannot relax; when we have work to do and can't concentrate; when we hear a siren in the night and wonder whose life has been touched by pain; when we are exhausted from work or emotional strain and a feeling of melancholy envelops us. "All things are wearisome," writes Qoheleth, but even in our weariness we are restless. We scan the next horizon. We chase after the wind.

When Gilgamesh, the brash young King of Uruk, was about to set out on a dangerous journey, his mother prayed to the goddess of the dawn: "Why was I given a son with a heart that will not rest?"

Her question might be asked by any mother. It is a question we might ask ourselves or one another. Why are we born with hearts that will not rest?

The yearning of the human heart also stirs in us at the changing of the seasons: When we watch buds opening in April, or leaves falling in October; when we become aware in a moment of disbelief that the days are gone, the weeks have slipped by, the months are torn off our calendars, and we really don't know where they have gone. We search the sky. We listen for the wind. We watch the leaves. We know that *these* leaves falling on *this* day will never come back again. Stephen Vincent Benét describes this emotion in his sketch of Ellyat, the young Yankee soldier in *John Brown's Body:* "(He) felt that turning of the year stir in his blood like drowsy fiddle music. . . ."[1]

The turning of the year. The stirring in the blood. The yearning in the heart. What are these? What is it that turns inside of us? What is it that stirs in our blood? What is this insatiable hunger of the human heart? The Greeks called it *nostos*—homesickness (whence comes "nostalgia"). The Vikings felt it as a wanderlust, the urge to explore what lay beyond the next horizon. Wordsworth referred to it as "intimations of immortality." Shakespeare described it as "immortal longings." Gerard Manley Hopkins compares the restless human self to an imprisoned lark:

> "As a dare-gale skylark scanted in a dull cage
> Man's mounting spirit in his bone-house, mean
> house, dwells—"[2]

Whatever description we choose to give it, the longing within us reveals an essential dimension of our lives: We are wayfarers who are still on the way. Our lives continue to be "unfinished business." We are incomplete. We lack something. We are not yet whole. We have not yet attained integrity. We strive for completion, for harmony, for meaning, for a fullness of life. A fullness—yes, that's it. A fullness. The term that we use most frequently today to describe the goal of our longing is "fulfillment." It is a good word. Full-fillment: It conveys at once the hunger within us and the destiny toward which we strive. It locates the human heart on the road of pilgrimage. "For every mile the feet walk," says E. E. Cummings, "the heart goes nine." The human heart is a nomad in search of eternal life. Each of us is like a window on eternity. We move in a room with a view overlooking the infinite. The vastness of outer space is a reality that is beyond our limited powers to calculate or even imagine. But the universe cannot be compared to the immense reaches of our inner selves. The human heart is deep space. Dag Hammarskjold reminds us in his *Markings* that "the longest journey is the journey inward." This is the journey we are making here—the inward journey in search of fulfillment, the pilgrimage toward the center of the self and the depth of life.

To reflect on the meaning of Christian fulfillment we must begin by exploring this hunger of the human heart. Fulfillment is the experience of wholeness, of completion, of totality. But we are born and we live in the condition of pilgrimage. We discover ourselves only in fragments and in fleeting glances. We are neither complete nor whole. Our work is never done. Our needs are never met. Our hearts are forever restless, our inward spirit groans with longing. We are nomads of the heart, and it is in the wilderness of the heart that the quest for fulfillment is born. The search for fullness begins with an awareness of our emptiness and the infinite openness of the human spirit.

If we were to meditate on the meaning of God's inner life we could begin with fulness. We could echo the opening words in John's gospel, "In the beginning was the Word." In the beginning, for God, there is power, there is creativity, there is the initiating act of self-communication and the gift of eternal love.

But for us it is different. If God is the word, we are the receptive ear, the listening heart. If God is the living bread, we are the hunger pangs of his creation. For us the story of life begins in another place. In the beginning is the ache. In the beginning is the restlessness. In the beginning is the yearning. In the beginning is the hunger.

The hunger of the human heart for fulfillment is as old as the dawn of consciousness. Poets and prophets, the seers and the wise have struggled to find a way to give creative expression to this yearning. They have tried to sing it into sound, to shape it into words, to give it feeling and form in dance and sculpture, in painting and pottery. In our day the search for fulfillment has also become the focus of the human sciences. It is the subject of research and experiment. It is studied in disciplines ranging from developmental psychology to urban planning.

Nowhere, I believe, has this restless hunger been given such eloquent and powerful expression as in the religious experience and the sacred writings of Judaism and Christianity. Where other religions offer ways of escaping from desire or of deadening the hunger as something illusory, the Judeo-Christian tradition nourishes the yearning of the human heart by directing it toward God. Scripture is the story of our hunger to know God. It is also the story of God's search to become our fullness.

In studying and praying the psalms, those songs of Israel's inward journey, I discover that I am not alone when I feel the flow of life near running streams. More than 2500 years ago on the banks of another river, a Hebrew poet tried to find words for

his longing. With his people, he was in exile somewhere in Babylonia, a stranger in a foreign land. His
hunger took the form of yearning to know familiar
faces, to see again the temple in Jerusalem, and to
walk the earth that he loved so much. We still sing
and pray his words in the haunting lyrics of
Psalm 42:

> As a doe longs
> for running streams
> so my soul
> longs for you, my God.
> My soul thirsts for God,
> the God of my life.
> When shall I go to see
> the face of God?

These lyrics give poetic expression to the longing
of the human heart for fulfillment. In the psalmist's
prayer we discover again that we are exiles. We are
looking for a way to come home to ourselves, to life,
and to God. The everyday prayer of the Hebrew
person nourished this longing for the fullness of life.
They named that fullness the face of God. The
Christian vision is likewise centered in the realization that only God can satisfy our inward thirst. The
goal of all our hunger is to experience communion
with the living God.

Like the deer that yearns. Like the earth that
groans. Like the heart that aches. Like the blood

that stirs. Like the river that moves. So does our
soul long for the fullness of God.

This yearning does not lead everyone to God. We
channel our restlessness in different ways. We have
differing levels of response to the hunger of our
hearts. Some of our responses lead us to the depth
of life, while others trap us into a mere surface
experience.

What do we do with the ache within us? How do
we respond to the turning of the year that stirs in
our blood? How do we respond to the feeling that we
are exiles?

Often, our first instinct is the desire to satisfy our
hunger with instantaneous gratification. We have
basic bodily and psychic needs. We are physically
hungry and thirsty. We yearn for peace of mind and
for feelings of security. We want to have control
over our lives. The possession of things that we can
master and control sometimes deceives us into
thinking that we have become "filled", that we have
found rest or that we are finished. This first temptation is the tendency to want to fill up the emptiness
within us. We overindulge in food or drink. We
overwork. We surround ourselves with more things,
more noise, more feverish activity. It is no accident
that in the United States we refer to ourselves as
"consumers." A consumer is literally someone who
uses things up. There is a growing concern to find

ways to protect our right to be consumers, to safe-guard the manner in which we use up reality. Herbert Marcuse, the neo-Marxist critic of American culture, contends that we are experiencing alienation today because we have deceived ourselves into thinking that we need more things, more conveniences, more apparatuses, more controls. Recently, we have even begun to refer to money as "bread." It is a revealing use of language. It tells us that we are depending on material things to nourish our inner lives. It tells us that we are confusing the good life with the easy life, the full life with the distracted life. We have traded personal values for consumer goods.

There are other ways that we look for short cuts to fulfillment. We can, for instance, try to fill up our lives with work. We place such high priority on being a functioning member of society that productivity becomes the measure of personal fulfillment. When it is time for retirement, people often feel discarded. They question whether their lives were meaningful because they are no longer considered useful by the rest of society. The attempt to find fulfillment exclusively in work can be an embittering experience in old age. When the test of life is productivity, retirement is equivalent to a death notice. The richness and wisdom of experience are forgotten, and in the evening of life the days that are gone seem empty and cold.

There is still another temptation. It is the urge to escape from or to deaden the hunger that is within us. When we cannot fill our emptiness immediately, we try to find ways to anaesthetize it. If we cannot stimulate ourselves by excitement, we try to tranquilize ourselves into forgetfulness. We look for ways to quiet the restlessness or to still the hunger.

These attempts to find short cuts to fulfillment do not lead to wholeness. They are experiences of frustration. They result not in fulfillment but in a deeper sense of emptiness and of alienation. Jesus once asked a question of those who followed him. It is a question that we need to hear again today: "What gain, then, is it for a man to win the whole world and ruin his life? And indeed what can a man offer in exchange for his life" (Mk 8:36-37)? In western society, we are learning that we have gained the whole world at the risk of losing our true selves. We have achieved technological mastery at the risk of losing our souls. We have sought a world of instant everything but we are not fulfilled. What we have not lost is the yearning, the ache and the longing.

There is a scene in John Updike's novel, *Rabbit Run*, in which the main character, Rabbit Angstrom, is on his way home after playing basketball with a group of high school boys. He jogs up an alley past a deserted ice plant, past . . . "ashcans, garage doors, fences of chickenwire, caging crisscrossing stalks of dead flowers. The month is March. Love makes the air light. Things start anew; Rabbit tastes through sour aftersmoke the fresh chance in the air. . . ."[3] Something of the hunger for life stirs in Rabbit. He realizes that there is always "a fresh chance." He senses that something out there is waiting for him to discover it. His journey, as the title suggests, becomes an aimless odyssey. The emptiness of his life compels him to flee. He is at once running and searching.

A similar kind of restlessness has surfaced in our society. Unlike Rabbit Angstrom's flight, our restlessness gives promise of having a more positive direction. There are signs of hope in our contemporary search for fulfillment. One of the most persistent signs is our growing awareness that there is a fresh chance, that there is something waiting for us to discover it. In contrast to Rabbit Angstrom, it is not so much "out there" as "in here." It is inside of us. It is part of the inner world of our feelings and possibilities.

In the past several years, we have experienced a revolt of the spirit. The youth rebellion of the sixties has not really disappeared. It has simply widened and deepened into a shared search for self-fulfillment. Men and women today are more self-conscious and more concerned about finding meaning in their lives than ever before. People today are more aware of their needs. They are also more sensitive to the dangerous ways in which they can short-circuit their own fulfillment. People want more than jobs today. They want to pursue a career. They want to take up a profession. The signs of this deeper quest for self-fulfillment are all about us: The interest in finding one's own way, the concern about human awareness, the neo-romanticism expressed in natural foods, hairstyles, and clothing. The quest for self-fulfillment manifests itself in our concern to be honest about our feelings, our values, and our convictions.

The new humanism is a healthy sign of this search for meaning. It reveals the ways in which we are in touch with the hunger of the human heart for something more, the awareness that something within us is waiting to be discovered.

But there are limitations to this human search. The emphasis on self-realization, self-actualization, and self-fulfillment can be subtle forms of narcissism. They can limit us to our personal needs and to the assumption that our possibilities are restricted to the human horizon. This concern for personal fulfillment can end in frustration. After the search for self-fulfillment, there is still the yearning. After all our attempts to meet our own needs there is still a hunger that is not satisfied, a restlessness that stirs in our blood. The search for personal fulfillment can put us in touch with our depths. It can help make us more real, more concerned about the things that really matter, but ultimately it cannot bring us true fulfillment.

The quest for self-fulfillment leads us to the edge of mystery. But what will lead us beyond the edge into the heart of that mystery? How can we go beyond the quest for self-fulfillment to a deeper experience of life?

For a Christian the answer is *faith*. Christianity offers us a revolution in awareness, a radical change in perspective. It provides us with an entirely new way of seeing. To believe is to find ourselves looking in a different place for fulfillment. Faith enables us to see, first, that our hunger is greater than anything our experience or our world can satisfy. Secondly, it enables us to accept that by our own efforts we cannot fulfill this infinite hunger. To put it simply, the Christian gospel tells us that fulfillment is not a human accomplishment, but a divine gift.

This discovery is at once the most painful and the most liberating of all conversions. It does not lessen, it rather increases our desire and our longing. At the same time, it frees us from the desire to fill up our hunger with material things and centers our thirst and our quest on God.

Beyond the search for self-fulfillment is the commitment to self-transcendence. The hunger of our hearts is greater than any ability we have to satisfy it. We are made for ecstasy. We are created for an experience of God. We are gifted with the infinite desire to be one with the Father. The most persistent human temptation is the tendency to take short cuts—to deny, to run from, to smother, or to drown the restlessness within us. We want to stop at the quest for self-fulfillment. But the call of faith will not allow us to rest there. Faith will not allow us to separate our personal search from our quest for God. In the introduction to his *Autobiography*, Gandhi describes this underlying unity of the human spirit as he experienced it in his life: "What I want to achieve—what I have been striving and pining to achieve these thirty years—is self-realization, to see God face to face. . . . I live and move and have my being in pursuit of this goal. All that I do by way of speaking and writing, and all my ventures into the political field, are directed to the same end."[4]

Christianity is an invitation to follow the hunger of the human spirit toward the infinite. Faith is the pathway that allows the immense restlessness within us to lead us toward the only source and goal that can satisfy our hearts: The living God.

Like the deer that yearns. Like the blood that stirs. Like the river that bends. Like the year that turns. Like the heart that longs. Like the soul that thirsts. So does our soul thirst for God, the God of our life. When shall we go to see the face of God?

FOOTNOTES

1. Stephen Vincent Benét, *Selected Works*, Vol. I, Poetry (New York: Farrar and Rinehart, 1942), p. 14.
2. Gerard Manley Hopkins, "The Caged Skylark," in *Poems and Prose of Gerard Manley Hopkins* (Baltimore: Penguin Books, 1968), p. 31.
3. John Updike, *Rabbit, Run* (New York: Fawcett World Library, 1969), p. 9.
4. M. K. Gandhi, *An Autobiography, The Story of My Experiments with Truth* (Boston: Beacon Press, 1968), p. xii.

Chapter Three

That They May Have Life

THE PROMISE OF THE GOSPEL

There is a story told about three men who were searching for the truth. In their travels they heard about a cave high in the mountains where a wise man lived in solitude. Rumor had it that this was the cave of truth. After a long journey, the travelers arrived at the cave. The wise man greeted them at the entrance.

"Before you enter the cave," he told them, "I must ask you one question: How far in do you want to go?"

The three men looked at one another for a moment. Then one of them responded: "Oh, not very far. Just far enough so we can say that we've been there."[1]

The cave, with its dark secrets, might be taken as a symbol of life. Its depths suggest an image of the human heart. We ourselves are the travelers. We are the seekers. We are hungry for the truth. We are on a journey in search of fulfillment. But as part of our luggage, we carry a set of expectations and fears. Our seeking is framed with conditions. We want to control the search and to set the limits of the journey. We want to create our own agenda for happiness. Of course we seek for the truth—but we demand it on our terms, and, if possible, without risk or pain.

As a result, many people pay life only a courtesy call. They approach human experience as though it were merely a tourist attraction. They come only as visitors. They travel as sightseers rather than as true pilgrims who are willing to walk into the mystery which is at the center of life. They take a few souvenirs at the edges and then return to safer ground. They come just far enough so they can say they've been there.

The desire to find personal fulfillment is the goal of many people today. But their search is often shallow and limiting. It is characterized by the same curiosity which led the men to the cave, but would not allow them to plumb its depths.

How far in do you want to go? This is the question that each of us must answer for ourselves. In the first stages of our search we are primarily concerned with meeting our own needs. We attempt to fill our lives with experiences that are pleasant and enriching. We are the focus of attention. Life is a search for my meaning, my happiness, my contentment. On this level, life is a pursuit of personal satisfaction. It is a quest for that elusive circumstance we call happiness.

But what would happen if we stopped being tourists and became pilgrims? What if we were willing to walk beyond the fringes of comfort into the depth of life? Where would it lead us? What would we discover?

This is precisely the invitation of the Christian gospel. Faith challenges us to go beyond a self-centered concern for fulfillment. It invites us to let go of our conditions and expectations and to embrace a deeper experience of life. Those who have made the journey toward the center of life are not remembered for the pleasure they experienced or the contentment they found. They are remembered for the fullness of life which they encountered. They are the saints and the sinners, the prophets and the mystics, the men and women of all ages who have walked with the vision of faith into the heart of the cave.

The existentialist philosopher, Karl Jaspers, describes certain moments in our lives when we are led to the edge of this deeper mystery. He refers to these occasions as "limit-situations." These are the times when we can no longer bargain with life or impose our conditions on its outcome. They are the moments of intensity and immediacy that defy our demand to be in control. We encounter "limit-situations" when we are faced with the sudden death of a loved one. When we wrestle with fears that are beyond our power to conquer. When we experience human love and the gift of unconditional acceptance. When our joy is too spontaneous to be contrived and too deep to be expressed.

At these moments something occurs within us that is capable of transforming our understanding of ourselves and of life. The yearning of our hearts reaches out beyond our personal needs toward a reality that we can neither control nor comprehend. Instead of making demands of life, we are surprised to find ourselves responding to life. We experience life as inviting us to something beyond our fears, beyond our need for security and the easy life. It is as though something at the heart of life is calling us by name, summoning us to abandon our narrow perimeter and to "cast out into the deep" (Lk 5:4).

Dag Hammarskjold describes this experience in *Markings:* "I don't know who—or what—put the question; I don't know when it was put. I don't even remember answering. But at some moment I did answer *Yes* to Someone—or Something—and from that hour I was certain that existence is meaningful and that, therefore, my life, in self-surrender, had a goal."[2]

I have reflected on these words of Hammarskjold many times. He expresses something that touches each of our lives. For me the important word is "self-surrender." It is at the moment of letting go that we win life. Self-surrender flows not from cowardice, but from courage. It is an act of power, not a gesture of passivity. It is the most dangerous and the most liberating of all human choices. Self-surrender is not giving in or giving up. It is opening up to the fearful energy of life. Only a person of vision and inner strength can grasp life with both hands, and then, with a leap of freedom, let go of it in order to be enveloped by its deeper mystery.

If we are willing to go beyond the shoreline of our personal desires and plunge into deep water, we will discover that life is richer and more powerful than we can imagine. At the moment of self-surrender we move from a concern for security to a spirit of adventure. At that moment we cease being tourists. We become pilgrims.

Dr. Viktor Frankl became a pilgrim during the three years he spent at Auschwitz and other Nazi prison camps. In his book, *Man's Search for Meaning*, Frankl recounts the horror and the agony of those years. His main concern was to describe the unwavering search for significance which he and his fellow prisoners shared. The prisoners were driven beyond basic needs—food, water, clothing—to a more fundamental level of existence, to the search for personal meaning. Even when the necessities of life were stripped from them, they continued to thirst for significance. As they struggled for meaning, a decisive transition began to take place in some of them. It involved the possibility of a conversion which could transform their values and their vision of life.

> "What was really needed was a fundamental change in our attitude toward life. We had to learn ourselves and, furthermore, we had to teach the despairing men that it really did not matter what we expected from life but rather what life expected from us. We needed to stop asking about the meaning of life and, instead, to think of ourselves as those who were being questioned by life—daily and hourly."[3]

These words contain the most important personal insight I have received from Frankl's writings. He captures the turning point in the Christian search for fulfillment. He is not speaking from a philosopher's lectern or from a research laboratory, but from *life*. He is describing human life in crisis. At this crossroad, fulfillment ceases to be a private quest. It becomes a shared response to the invitation of God. It ceases to be something *we* achieve. It becomes a gift we receive, a summons to which we respond in faith. The implications of this change in perspective are momentous. We must understand them clearly.

We are born with a restless hunger in our hearts. We grow up with the desire to satisfy our yearning, to fill up our emptiness. This longing stirs in us ceaselessly. We can choose to smother it with passing gratification or to deaden it with distraction. We can choose to stay at the edges of life. We can continue to be tourists. But if we follow our thirst for fulfillment far enough, it will lead us beyond self-fulfillment to self-transcendence. It will lead us to the awareness that beyond hunger is invitation.

This is the moment of conversion. We discover that we who are seekers are, in turn, being sought. Life is addressing us. We are being called by name. As we move toward the center of the cave we discover that we are responders even before we are seekers. Our lives are more than tasks we perform or roles we play, more even than professions or careers that we pursue. Life is a vocation. From the depth of life there comes a call. Life is not a monologue; it is a dialogue. It is not just a quest; it is an encounter.

What is it in life that is addressing us? Where does the invitation come from? What is the meaning of the call? Christianity tells us that the source of the call is more than just an impersonal cosmic power. It is not just a hidden form of fate. Faith reveals that the call originates in a personal presence who invites us into a relationship of trust and love. It is the living God who calls us by name. In the depth of the cave there is love. At the heart of life there is a meeting with the Father.

Christian fulfillment can only be understood in terms of this invitational quality of human life. The starting point of the Christian vision of fullness is the realization that the hunger in our hearts is beyond anything we can do to satisfy it. If we follow our hunger it will lead us to God. At the center of life there is an encounter and a relationship. God has spoken the first word. He has begun the conversation. Before we are aware of him, God initiates a dialogue of love with us.

What Frankl describes in his prison experience, the Christian gospel speaks of as an event in every person's life. In the gospel, the invitation of life becomes immediate and personal. It is centered in the experience and presence of Jesus.

There is a scene in the gospel of John which describes the turning point in a Christian's quest for fulfillment. It is a story of hunger. It is a story of seeking. It is a story of invitation and dialogue.

Jesus is about to begin his public life. It is a time of transition. It is a moment of inward searching. It is a time of new beginnings.

He has lived a carpenter's life. He has lived what centuries later we would call "the hidden years." During these years Jesus drank deeply of the human condition. Like all of us, he searched for the meaning of his life. He reached out for fulfillment. St. Luke says simply that Jesus "grew in wisdom, in stature, and in favor with God and men" (Lk 2:52). But growth does not come easily. To grow is to grope, to question, to wonder, and, sometimes, to get lost. The gospel doesn't tell us much about Jesus' inward struggle during this time. There is only one incident—the occasion when Jesus remained in Jerusalem after his parents and relatives had left for home. This is a portrait of the young, searching Jesus. It is a significant description of his inward journey.

There must have been other times when Jesus struggled with his mission and his identity. There must have been other moments when he was not understood by his family, his friends, and his neighbors. "Did you not know that I must be about my Father's business?" This is the question of a searching heart. A hunger stirred in him. A presence called to him from the depths of his being. During these years the call to be about his Father's business continued to haunt him.

Now it is time. Now it is the hour to do the Father's work. Jesus comes out of the Jordan with a new awareness of the Father's love. He comes out of the desert with a restlessness to share the experience of the spirit which stirs in him. Now, at the turning point of his life, in the consuming fire of his zeal, Jesus decides to follow his truth to the depths.

Jesus begins to walk the roads and hills of Pales-

tine. He preaches as any other young rabbi might,
but with an intensity and a depth of conviction that
startles the crowds.

One day two men follow Jesus down the road.
Their names are John and Andrew. They are fishermen by trade, but the nets and the sea are not
enough for them. They are looking for something
more. They, too, are seekers. They, too, are
hungry. When Jesus becomes aware of their presence, he turns and asks them, "What do you want"
(Jn 1:38)? His question seems to be one of curiosity,
but it has deeper implications. Jesus is asking the
two fishermen about their vision and their values.
What do you seek from life? What are you really
looking for? What is the deepest desire of your
heart? How far in do you want to go?

John and Andrew might have given any of the
answers that people have given throughout history.
They might have asked for possessions and riches.
They might have demanded to become powerful or
famous. They might have requested a life free from
care. Instead, their answer took the form of another
question, "Where do you live?"

Like Jesus, they have moved beyond the level of
curiosity. They are not asking about geography or
the location of Jesus' house. They are not just
making conversation. They are asking about life.
Their search has led them beyond possessions,

beyond fishing nets and boats, beyond jobs and careers. Their question is more of why and how than of where. We might rephrase it to read: What are you about? What is the meaning of your life? They found in Jesus the beginning of something more. In him they heard a call from the heart of life.

Jesus responds to their question with a simple invitation: "Come and see." He doesn't give them material goods to fill their hunger. He doesn't give them formulas with which to satisfy their yearning. He doesn't present them with a set of teachings or a list of ethical rules. He simply invites them to come and share life with him. He invites them to enter into a relationship, to become part of a community and a way of life.

Christianity is an invitation to come and see. It is a call to a shared journey and to a vision of life. It is an invitation to move from the periphery toward the center, from the surface to the depth. It is a call to discover God in the cave of human life.

The hunger of the human heart leads us to a road. It urges us to undertake a pilgrimage. Along the way, we catch up with a Stranger. He turns and asks us, "What do you want?" We have no words with which to answer for our hunger is immense. We ask him, in turn, "Where do you live?" "Come and see," he says, and the dialogue of faith begins.

Faith is the foundation of the Christian understanding of fulfillment. It is faith that enables us to risk entering the depth of life. It is faith which enables us to discover that God has come in search of us. Once we discover that life is asking questions of us, once we become aware of the invitational quality of human experience, we must respond in some way to the call.

Invitations are common experiences. Some of them make us happy. Some of them make us uncomfortable. One thing is clear. We must *do* something with an invitation. We can welcome the opportunity and say, "Yes," or we can reject the invitation and say, "No thank you." We cannot simply ignore an invitation. To ignore it is another way of rejecting it. The same is true with the invitation of faith. Jesus calls us into a relationship of fidelity and love. We can accept his invitation or reject it, but we cannot ignore it.

"Come and see," says Jesus to John and Andrew. They not only respond to his invitation, they share it with others. Andrew tells his brother, Simon Peter. Peter tells his friend, Philip. Philip finds Nathaniel and says to him, "We have found the one Moses wrote about in the law, the one about whom the prophets wrote. He is Jesus, son of Joseph, from Nazareth." "From Nazareth," said Nathaniel. "Can anything good come from that place?" "Come and see," replied Philip (Jn 1:45-46). The invitation is spreading. Philip used the same words as Jesus to call others. In John's gospel, the first disciples are the first recruiters for the kingdom.

It is only the beginning. Soon, people come from all over Galilee, Judea, and the surrounding countryside to see Jesus and to listen to his message. They come with all the hungers that are part of human life. They come seeking to be filled in many different ways. Some are hungry for food, some are blind or lame or hunched over or possessed. Some are hungry for healing. Some are looking for signs and wonders. Some come out of need, others out of curiosity.

Jesus is surrounded by crowds, but he reaches out to individuals. In each instance, he sees into their eyes and through their eyes into their hearts. He understands that their hungers are deeper than they know. He sees beneath the surface into their restless hearts.

Nicodemus comes to him by night, seeking for answers. Jesus invites him to go beneath the surface of his life and to discover there the need for rebirth.

Jesus encounters a Samaritan woman at the well of Jacob. He initiates a conversation with her by asking her for a drink of water. Then he leads her to the deeper thirst for living water. He invites her to go beyond her quest for self-fulfillment and to discover God's invitation to life.

The son of a court official is dying. "Go home," Jesus tells him. "Your son will live" (Jn 4:49). In his encounter with Jesus the official is reborn in faith. He has heard the call at the depth of life. The father is healed before the son.

A man has been paralyzed for thirty-eight years. He waits helplessly for the waters of the Sheep Pool to move. He knows that he has no way of reaching them. "Do you want to be well again?" Jesus asks him (Jn 5:7). The source of living water stands at his side. Jesus reaches out to touch him. "Get up, pick up your sleeping mat and walk."

Jesus responds to crowds in the same way that he approaches individuals. When they are discouraged and without hope, he tells them of his Father's love for them. When they are hungry and weary, he tries to meet their needs. He feeds them with loaves and fishes and invites them to rest. But he doesn't stop with their immediate needs. Their hunger for loaves is only the beginning. He calls them to a deeper hunger, a deeper thirst. When they demand that he become a wonder worker and a giver of bread, when they try to make Jesus into a person who will continue to satisfy only their immediate needs, he confronts them. "I tell you most solemnly, you are not looking for me because you have seen the signs but because you had all the bread you wanted to eat. Do not work for food that cannot last, but work for food that endures to eternal life, the kind of food the Son of Man is offering you, for on him, the Father, God himself, has set his seal" (Jn 6:26-27).

As Jesus' relationship with his followers deepens, his invitation to come and see becomes clearer and more urgent. The call becomes a pledge. The invitation becomes a promise.

What is the promise of the gospel? What awaits us if we respond to the invitation of Jesus? Why has he drawn near to our lives?

"I have come that they may have life and have it to the full" (Jn 10:10). Life to the full. This is the promise of the gospel. This is the pledge that Jesus makes to his disciples. Life to the full. This is the Christian word for fulfillment. The gospel does not speak of fulfillment in the familiar way we use the term today. The gospel speaks of *life*—fullness of life. For Christianity, fulfillment is not an end in itself, but an overflow of life. Fulfillment comes as a result of a life that is lived in faith and love. Fulfillment is like a jet stream across the sky. It tells us that a source of life and energy, a presence of great power has passed by. Christians do not pursue fulfillment—they seek life, and with the gift of life comes everything. "Seek first the kingdom of heaven, and all else will be given to you besides" (Mt 6:33).

Jesus also describes the promise of fulfillment in his use of the term "eternal life". The son of man has come, Jesus says to Nicodemus, "So that everyone who believes in him may not be lost but may have eternal life" (Jn 3:16). He tells the woman at the well, "Whoever drinks this water will get thirsty again, but anyone who drinks the water that I shall give will never be thirsty again: The water that I shall give will turn into a spring inside him, welling up to eternal life" (Jn 4:14). To the Jews, who objected to Jesus healing on the Sabbath, he said, "Whoever listens to my words and believes in the one who sent me, has eternal life" (Jn 5:24). To the crowds who came looking for food, Jesus says, "I am the bread of life. He who comes to me will never by hungry. He who believes in me will never thirst" (Jn 6:35).

Christianity is not only an invitation. It is a promise. It is a promise with implications. Christianity is good news, but it is not easy news. Those who come to Jesus to meet only their physical or emotional needs find themselves challenged to a deeper experience of life. They hear promises they cannot understand. They hear words that are difficult to accept.

If we follow our hunger far enough we will hear an invitation. If we respond to the invitation long enough we will learn of the promise. If we follow the promise, we will be confronted with the implications. Jesus challenges us with what Dietrich Bonhoeffer calls the "cost of discipleship." The promise of the gospel points us toward Jerusalem. It leads us to the garden and to a place called Golgotha.

How far in do you want to go? At some point in the journey of faith, each of us must answer this question.

The implications of the gospel constitute the greatest challenge to our faith. The promise of eternal life demands that we die to ourselves, that we let go of life, that we break through the surface and walk toward the depth. This is the reason why many people look upon the Christian life and personal fulfillment as contradictory. Many see Christianity as a way of self-denial rather than a way of self-fulfillment. In a limited sense, they are correct, but they do not see deeply enough. They do not see that the call to die to self is actually a call to receive the fullness of life.

Today, as in the time of Jesus, the gospel is a "hard saying." Those who come to see must decide about the implications of their search.

In Jesus' life this turning point comes after the multiplication of the loaves. Jesus tells the crowds that they must seek a different kind of food. They must become totally involved in his life. "I am the living bread which has come down from heaven.

Anyone who eats this bread will live forever and the bread that I shall give is my flesh for the life of the world" (Jn 6:50-51). When the Jews question him, Jesus responds directly: "I tell you most solemnly, if you do not eat the flesh of the son of man and drink his blood, you will not have life in you" (Jn 6:53). The gospel summons us to be so united with Christ that we die with him. This is what makes Christianity a hard saying. "After this, many of his disciples left him and stopped going with him" (Jn 6:66).

As the crowds begin to walk away, Jesus turns to his closest friends. He sees the puzzled look on their faces. He knows that they, too, are wondering. He asks them simply, "Will you also go away?" He is asking them the question with which we began this meditation. "How far in do you want to go?" Are you still willing to keep on walking toward the center of life?"

At first there is a bewildered silence. Then Peter, who is usually impetuous and has ready answers, responds quietly for the others. This time he is neither impetuous, nor is he sure. "Lord, to whom can we turn? You alone have the words of eternal life" (Jn 6:67).

There was a time when I believed that Peter's response was a half-hearted act of faith. I no longer believe this. In our time, we also experience Christianity as a hard saying. Each of us wrestles with

the question of Jesus, "Will you also go away?" Each
of us struggles to move deeper into the pilgrimage
of faith. We live in a world in which many people
want fulfillment without implications. They seek for
happiness without cost. They are content to remain
tourists. They want to live only enough of life to be
able to say that they have been there.

The invitation and the promise of the gospel continue to challenge us. We are invited to cast our lot
with Jesus. What I once thought was a weak act of
faith for Peter, I now recognize as a radical commitment. Like Peter, we have no easy answers to the
hard saying of Christianity. We have no simple way
of explaining to the rest of the world that the gospel
is a way of fulfillment. We cannot always give a
clear answer to the Lord's question of whether or
not we intend to keep on walking. But we can make
Peter's act of faith our own. "Lord, to whom can we
turn? You alone have the words of life."

FOOTNOTES

1. This story is based on material in James W. Douglas, *Resistance and Contemplation* (New York: Doubleday, 1972), p. 46. He, in turn, refers to the comments of Bob Dylan on the record jacket of his album, *John Wesley Harding.* I have changed the parable considerably, but I am indebted to these sources for its main point.
2. Dag Hammerskjold, *Markings* (New York: Afred A. Knopf, 1965), p. 205.
3. Viktor E. Frankl, *Man's Search for Meaning* (New York: Pocket Books—Simon & Schuster, 1963), p. 122.

Chapter Four

He Emptied Himself

THE RISK OF OPENNESS

One of the most poignant scenes in the gospel is the encounter between Jesus and the rich young man. As Jesus was about to leave on a journey a young man came to him and asked, "Good Master, what must I do to inherit eternal life?" Jesus recounted the great commandments of the Law. When he had finished, the young man assured him that he had observed them from his childhood. "Jesus looked steadily at him and loved him, and he said, 'There is one thing you lack. Go and sell everything you own and give the money to the poor, and you will have treasure in heaven; then come, follow me.' But his face fell at these words and he went away sad, for he was a man of great wealth" (Mk 10:21-22).

This is a disturbing story for me. Like Jesus, I, too, am drawn to the young man. There is something attractive, even familiar about him. He is a seeker of life. He is a person with values and strong convictions. He takes life seriously. I recognize my own restlessness in him—the desire to grow, the search for deeper meaning, the yearning for something more.

But at what price? This is the question. Like Jesus, I have gazed steadily at the young man. I have discovered something of myself in him. Something in his fallen countenance. Something in his manner as he turns to walk away. Something of the sadness that comes from clinging to life with hesitating hands.

The story of the young man in the gospel came to life for me when I witnessed a similar encounter. At the height of the civil rights movement, Martin Luther King was addressing a large rally in support of the 1964 Civil Rights Act. After his speech he was surrounded by a crowd of admirers. A young college student pushed her way through the crowd until she was close enough to talk to the black leader. She told him about her work for civil rights. She told him how discouraged she was with the lack of results. Finally, she asked, "What difference am I really making? How can I know if my life has meaning?" Without hesitating, Dr. King responded, "Your life will have meaning on the day you have found something worth living for that is so important you'd die for it."

Both the gospel story and this contemporary encounter describe the search for fulfillment. The rich young man and the student are really asking the same question: What can I do to achieve success? What are the essential conditions of happiness? How can I find personal fulfillment?

These questions express real issues. Both the young man and the student want to know the truth. They are not trying to test those they question. They are seeking to understand. They are good people who want to know that their lives make a difference.

What is missing? What is the one thing that is lacking?

The missing dimension is a spirit of self-surrender. They are not willing to let go of everything and receive life as a gift. I am attracted to them because their questions are close to my own. Their search is my search. What they lack is what is missing in most of our lives—the willingness to go the whole way.

What must I do to inherit eternal life? How can I know if my life has meaning? We assume that the answer to these questions has something to do with public acts of achievement. We picture success in terms of tangible results—a project brought to completion, a cause that moves thousands, a name that will be remembered. It is true that Jesus demands commitment and personal involvement. But the "one thing lacking" is not, first of all, an action, it is an inward attitude. We think that fulfillment is

something we must do. Jesus tells us it is something
we *are*, something we must become. The essential
condition of gaining eternal life is an inner conviction. It is the willingness to let go of everything,
even of success, in order to receive the gift of life
from the Father. This essential condition can be put
into one word. The one thing lacking is *openness.*

Openness is the risk we take for the sake of the
kingdom. It is the treasure waiting in the field of our
lives, the pearl of great price. Once we have discovered it, we can let go of everything else. We
have found what is missing. We have discovered the
one thing that is lacking. Openness is the expansive-
ness of a heart that has no more locks, no more
barriers. It is the reason Ghandi became known as
"The Mahatma"—the great soul. Like Jesus, like
Martin Luther King, like the other prophets,
Ghandi loved life deeply enough to release his grasp
on it, and become truly free.

Openness is also a call to vulnerability. It is the
willingness to give up our claims to security, our
demands, our carefully constructed means of pro-
tection. "Anyone who wants to save his life must
lose it; but anyone who loses his life for my sake,
and for the sake of the gospel, will save it" (Mk
8:36).

To be vulnerable literally means to be "capable of
being wounded." Vulnerability is the most costly

commitment in Christian life. It is what led Jesus to the cross, and beyond the cross to new life. The fear of vulnerability is the reason why so many of us walk away from Christianity with sadness. We are afraid of the wounds. We have too much to lose. We cling to our position of security.

In his letter to the Christians at Philippi, St. Paul preserves an early Christian hymn. It is the hymn of Jesus, the suffering servant. It is a song of vulnerability. It is a portrait of openness: "In your minds you must be the same as Christ Jesus:

> His state was divine
> yet he did not cling
> to his equality with God
> but emptied himself
> to assume the condition of a slave
> and became as men are;
> and being as all men are,
> he was humbler yet,
> even to accepting death,
> death on a cross.
> But God raised him high
> and gave him the name
> which is above all other names
> so that all beings
> in the heavens, and on earth and in the underworld,
> should bend the knee at the name of Jesus
> and that every tongue should acclaim
> Jesus Christ as Lord,
> to the glory of God the Father" (Ph. 2:5-11).

He emptied himself. The Christian way to fulfillment is an invitation to live in the tension of this paradox. It finds life by releasing it. It begins with the risk of openness and vulnerability. It reaches out to what St. Paul describes as the "madness" of the cross.

This commitment to openness is a contradiction to the accepted way of pursuing fulfillment. We must face this contradiction if we are to take responsibility for its consequences in our lives.

There are two basic ways that fulfillment is sought in our world. Both of these ways represent selective openness to life. They are low in personal risk and high in the demands and controls they put on life. We recognize them as patterns that play like shadows across our lives.

We might describe them as "the way of desire" and the "way of duty." In the first, the way of desire, we seek for happiness by satisfying our needs. In the second, the way of duty, we try to find fulfillment by proving ourselves through work and personal accomplishments.

The way of desire is sometimes pictured in the caricature of the person who drops out of society to "do his own thing." His life is a search for that experience which satisfies his needs with the least amount of personal investment. He abandons responsibility to seek for excitement.

The second option, the way of duty, is often pictured in the straight-looking business executive who commutes to his office each morning, briefcase in hand, reading *The Wall Street Journal.* His life is his work. His goal is his career. His measure of fulfillment is his list of accomplishments, his salary, and his promotions.

These are two stereotypes of the way in which many people seek for fulfillment. Most of us live somewhere between these two extremes. We live with an unresolved tension. We fluctuate between following our desires and doing our duty. As different as these two perspectives seem to be, they have something in common. They both assume that fulfillment is something we do for ourselves. Both the way of desire and the way of duty seek to maintain control over life. Whether we grasp at fulfillment or try to earn it, our lives remain closed to the deeper call of the gospel. We walk away sad, because our main concern is personal security. We demand life on our terms. We are not yet fully open to the depth of human life or to the invitation to let go of everything.

I want to illustrate these two extremes by reflecting on a familiar story—the parable of the prodigal son. This story is usually interpreted as a parable of mercy and forgiveness. I want to approach it as a parable of the quest for fulfillment.

When discussed as a story of forgiveness, it is the younger son, the "prodigal," who is the central character. When we reflect on it as a story of fulfillment, there are three leading characters—the younger son, his older brother, and the father. Each of them represents a different way of approaching fulfillment. The dramatic tension of the story arises in the contrast between the two brothers and the opposing manner in which they seek for happiness. The younger brother follows the way of desire. The older brother follows the way of duty. The father goes beyond these two attitudes. He approaches fulfillment as a gift to be shared and celebrated. Let's look more closely at the way each of them seeks for fulfillment.

First, there is the younger brother. He is the rebel, the dropout. He is the restless seeker of fortune. The younger brother is the most popular character in the story because he appeals to our imagination and to our spirit of adventure. He represents the person who believes that fulfillment is found in the excitement of life. Take your inheritance and see the world. Break loose from the deadening routine of duty and work. Be yourself. Try everything.

The younger brother's journey ends in disaster. When his money is gone so are his possibilities of experiencing life as he understands it. Gone, too, are his passing relationships and his self-confidence. His quest for fulfillment ends with these ironic words: "And he would willingly have filled his belly with the husks the pigs were eating but no one offered him anything" (Lk 15:16). The younger brother's attempt to follow the way of desire ends in emptiness and despair. But in his despair, there is a moment of conversion. The gospel says simply, "he came to himself." In this moment of "homecoming" his way of thinking and searching—his whole life— is turned around. Because he has come home to his deeper self, he is ready to come home to his father.

Then, there is the older brother. Often he is either left out of the story or he is looked upon as unimportant. Actually, he is as significant as the younger brother. He is not as popular or as appeal- ing because he seems so ordinary. He is like most of us. He represents those who look upon fulfillment as something to be earned by hard work and deter- mination. For him success is a contract we make with life. If we keep the rules, if we do our job, then recognition and fulfillment will follow.

The older brother is not unlike the rich young man. Both of them kept the rules from childhood. Both were responsible members of society. They had lists of accomplishments and material posses- sions to prove it.

Perhaps we want to ignore the older brother

because we are uncomfortable with him. We see too much of ourselves in him. He reflects the way in which many of us approach fulfillment. He also mirrors the way we understand our relationship with God. The older brother reveals an attitude toward the Christian life which denies natural desires and forces human life into a mold of duty and fear. For the older brother, desire is the forbidden dimension of life. Duty is its daily task.

His stance, like that of the younger brother, is closed to life. The older brother does his work, but he finds no happiness in it. He performs his duty, but he resents it. His mind and heart are somewhere else. He gives a detailed description of his younger brother's adventures even though neither his father nor his brother had told him about them. The older brother made the journey of desire many times, but only in his imagination. He lived and worked with envy and bitterness. Doing his duty had not destroyed his desire, it had only changed it into hatred.

The older brother is dead inside. He has lost his sense of wonder. There is no room left in his life for surprise or celebration. He weighs everything on scales. He wants life written out in the form of a contract. He is as empty inside as his younger brother was at the lowest point of his journey.

But the younger brother was converted. His life

was turned around. He came home. The older
brother remains alienated from life. Unlike his
younger brother, he does not come to himself. We
don't know if the older brother ever came in from
the fields.

Both the younger and the older brother represent
selective ways of seeking fulfillment. They sym-
bolize our desire to have happiness on our terms
rather than as a gift from God.

Finally, there is the father. From the perspective
of Christian fulfillment, he is the hero of the story.
He is the leading character. In the end, this is not
the parable of the prodigal son or the dutiful
brother. It is the story of the loving father. It is the
story of an open man who is free enough to share life
as a gift. His only concern is to reconcile his sons to
life and to themselves. He wants to welcome them
to the table of love.

The character of the father is revealed in his
relationship with his sons. He believes that fulfillment is realized in freely giving and receiving love.
He goes out to meet his sons in the same spirit of
openness with which he reaches out to life. When
his younger son returns, the father does not question him. He will not even allow him to finish his
well-rehearsed statement of repentance. He simply
welcomes him home and calls for a celebration.

In the same way, the father goes out into the

fields to reassure his older son. He reminds him that he has the right and privilege of inheritance: "My son, you are with me always and all I have is yours" (Lk 15:31).

Life is a gift. It is not something we can grasp or earn. It waits to be received in openness and shared in love. To receive the gift of life and to share it is another word for fulfillment. Fulfillment is the overflow of life's welcome and abundance. Where there is shared life there is also a spirit of festivity. "But it was only right we should celebrate and rejoice, because your brother here was dead and has come to life; he was lost and is found" (Lk 15:32).

The father embodies the Christian way to fulfillment. In telling this story, Jesus shares his experience of his Father's love. He communicates his view of life. It is a revolutionary vision of fulfillment. It is good news. The gospel tells us that we do not have to choose between desire and duty. Fulfillment transcends both need and obligation. If we follow our desire into the depth of life we will encounter a loving father: "Bring the calf we have been fattening . . . we are going to have a feast." If we go beyond our duty we will discover that our lives are gifts. "My son, you are with me always and all that I have is yours." In Christian discipleship desire and duty are transformed into joyful love. Our deepest desire is to love God. Our most urgent duty is to let

go of life. "Teach us to care and not to care," writes
T. S. Eliot. "Teach us to sit still." Openness is the
stillness that flows from trust. It is the spirit of
attentive love. It is a listening heart.

Openness must permeate our search for fulfillment. In the gospels, Jesus suggests three stages in
our growth toward openness.

First, Jesus speaks of the value of childlikeness:
"Unless you become as little children, you cannot
enter the kingdom of heaven." We are born open to
life, We come into life in a state of dependency and
need. Children experience life without the filter of
fear and suspicion. They cry about their needs.
They sleep without anxiety. They look in wonder at
a shaft of morning light. They are awestruck by the
world.

Wonder is the emotion of openness. "A man who
does not wonder," writes Thomas Carlyle, "is like a
pair of spectacles behind which there are no eyes."
When we no longer see with the eyes of the heart
we become calculating and deliberative. We are
blind to beauty. We miss the surprises that are
everywhere in creation.

The openness of children also makes them vulnerable. Children learn from pain as well as from love.
They are open enough to experience life in its falls
and bruises. They have not yet built walls to protect
themselves from the dark side of human experience.

The second level of openness is the call to maturity. Jesus praises the childlike qualities of simplicity and trust. Yet he does not invite his disciples to remain children. He is talking about a quality of the heart that must be a lasting dimension of our growth. Childlikeness is different from childishness.

This second level of openness is the growth toward adulthood. Christianity is a call to grow up. It is a challenge to walk the mature road of faith, to respond to the time of discipleship and decision. A mature Christian keeps a receptive heart and a contemplative spirit as the source of his commitment. "Be innocent as doves but clever as serpents," Jesus tells his followers. The Christian way to fulfillment is a combination of toughness and openness, of innocence and insight. Discipleship is the journey toward a deeper trust and a more radical commitment. Our vulnerability opens us to suffering. Our mature commitment leads us to the cross. Even as we take up the cross there is a need for a childlike spirit. There is a call to laughter all along the road to Jerusalem. Daniel Berrigan says it well: "If you cannot live in the horse's mouth, you will probably never make it in the lion's den." Christians are willing to be "lifted up," both on the cross and in resurrection, because they have learned that trust is a decision as well as a state of mind.

There is a third level of openness in the Christian road toward fulfillment. It is the level of freely chosen surrender to the Father. In one sense it is a return to the trust and simplicity of a child. In another sense it is the highest form of freedom, the most decisive act of responsibility. It takes us beyond both childlike trust and adult responsibility to Christian love. It is what Jesus describes to the rich young man as the "one thing lacking." It is the total openness of Jesus on the cross: "Father, into your hands I commend my spirit."

At that moment, Jesus was at once totally dependent and totally decisive. He was completely helpless and yet fully free. He was at once Son and Lord, Lamb and Shepherd. He gathered his life together in freedom to release it in love. He let go of everything. He emptied himself.

In the growth from childlike faith to mature commitment we are challenged to take charge of our lives and to clarify our values. The emphasis on the adult level of openness is that of responsibility. But the paradox of the gospel is that the highest form of freedom is self-surrender. The highest form of responsibility is to become totally open to the Father. It is to return to the vulnerability of a child through the mature freedom of an adult.

The "little ones" of which Jesus speaks in the gospel are more than children. They are the *anawim*

—the poor ones of God's people—the outcast, the forgotten, the gentle but strong people who follow God across the desert into the dark night of faith. They are Mary and Elizabeth. They are Joseph and Zechariah. They are Anna and Simeon. They are the shepherds who watch for stars in the night. They are the people of the beatitudes—the meek, the humble, the simple of heart, the mourning, the questors for justice and the seekers of peace. The strength which makes them both innocent and clever, trusting and decisive, is the gift of openness.

They do not walk away sad. They discover the one thing lacking. They find something worth living for that is so important they are willing to die for it. They come home to the Father's feast of love. In emptying themselves they discover the fullness of life.

Chapter Five

With the Holy Spirit and With Fire

THE ENERGY OF LIFE

The night air stirs. Along the ridges there is the sound of rustling leaves. The first murmur of morning. A nighthawk takes flight. He catches the edge of a breeze and rides it down the valley through fields of ripening grain. With the wind comes a feeling of expectancy. *There is creativity in the air.*

In the east, where there was only a hint of light, there is now an expanding band of dawn. Here and there the sky breaks into streaks of morning color. Then, without a sound, and with growing brilliance, the sun rises. *There is fire in the sky.*

In the rolling hills of Wisconsin, where I grew up, this is the sound and scenery of morning. For me, it is more than a sketch of dawn. It is a way of seeing, an experience of insight. Our vision is shaped by our surroundings. The earth and the sky of our childhood never leave us. We carry them with us as memories and metaphors. They shape our language and our way of understanding. Even when our minds move into the world of abstraction, our memory still runs barefoot in the dew.

The wind and the sun. The breath and the fire. Every morning these sources of creativity move across the land in a daily cycle that brings life and movement, growth and harvest to our lives.

Creation is God's first way of speaking to us. Each dawn tells us something about life and our hunger for fulfillment. St. Bonaventure refers to the world as "the footprints of God." The footprints leave a pattern. They create a shape. They reveal a theme. When we view life through the eyes of faith, this pattern speaks to us of the inward quest for fulfillment. From the wind and the sun we learn something of the breath and fire of God. Like the earth, the human heart moves toward life by becoming open and receptive. We are invited to become good soil. We are called to open ourselves to God's creative wind and to his purifying flame. "As the rain and the snow come down from the heavens and do not return without watering the earth, making it yield and giving growth to provide seed for the sower and bread for the eating, so the word that goes from my mouth does not return to me empty, without carrying out my will and succeeding in what it was sent to do" (Is 55:10-11).

In the beginning is the hunger. In the night is the

call. In the morning is the promise. But during the
day there is the journey. During the day there is the
work of creation. The hunger, the call, and the
promise of fulfillment grow slowly. They mature
only through inward struggle. Before there can be
fullness of life there must be openness of heart. Into
that openness God sends the wind and the fire. He
sends the Spirit to create and to purify. When we
open our lives to God, when we remove the walls of
fear, then the Spirit comes to breathe in us.

The wind and the fire are scriptural images of
God's creative presence. They move through the
world and through our lives to lead creation toward
fulfillment. The Church expresses these biblical
images in the prayer to the Holy Spirit: "Come Holy
Spirit, fill the hearts of your faithful and enkindle in
them the fire of your divine love. Send forth your
spirit and they shall renew the face of the earth."
This is a prayer for fulfillment. It reveals the pattern with which God creates life. Into a situation of
openness and receptivity, where there are un-
shaped possibilities, God comes to create. This pattern is present throughout the history of God's relationship with his people. It is like a thread weaving a
tapestry of life and growth. Our lives are the fabric
out of which this tapestry continues to be created.

This meditation is a reflection on the biblical back-
ground of this creative pattern. It is an exploration

of the ways in which God's creative breath and purifying flame are part of our growth toward fulfillment.

The book of Genesis opens with these words: "In the beginning, God created the heavens and earth. Now the earth was a formless void, there was darkness over the deep, and God's Spirit hovered over the water" (Gn 1:1-2). These words are like the opening movement of a great symphony. They state a theme. They sound a chord. They proclaim the pattern of God's creative presence in the world.

The author of Genesis is not presenting an abstract discussion on the topic of creation from nothingness. He is neither a scientist nor a philosopher. He is a poet. He is an artist who feels the drama of creation as an experience in human life. He is a composer who seeks to orchestrate the awesome power and beauty of God's creative energy. He seeks to find music for an unfinished symphony.

Genesis employs two words to describe the condition of the world before God sent his Spirit. These two words can be translated as "a trackless waste and emptiness."[1] It is over this dark and chaotic womb that the Spirit of God begins to move. In Hebrew the word for spirit is *ruah*. Depending on the context, *ruah* can mean wind, breath, or spirit. Each of these—wind, breath, and spirit—is an energy which finds its source in the creative power of God. Thus, the *ruah* of God is the primordial wind that sweeps across the dark abyss at the beginning of time. It hovers over the primeval chaos to create order and harmony. The *ruah* of God is also the divine breath that creates life in its own image. When God breathes into the clay he transforms it into a living being called man. Finally, the *ruah* of God is the divine spirit which is the life-source of all creation, from the smallest cell to the whirling suns and stars of the universe. "The spirit of the Lord fills the whole world. It holds all things together and knows every word spoken by man" (Ws 1:7).

The wind of creation. The breath of life. The spirit of the Lord. These biblical images reveal a central theme of creativity. They tell us that God is more than the fullness of life. They reveal that he is the self-communicating *source* of life. God is essentially, but freely creative. He moves through the trackless waste of creation to shape and form, to enliven and purify, to expand and fulfill the infinite possibilities of life.

The theme which is sounded in the creation story is developed in the liberation event of Exodus. The Israelites are in slavery, not only physically but spiritually. Egypt symbolizes the return of creation to the abyss, to human chaos. It is a trackless wasteland of the spirit. It is a wilderness without hope.

But the hunger for life still broods in a slave's

heart. It expresses itself as a longing for freedom and self-identity. This restlessness drives a man named Moses into the desert. There he encounters the fire. The consuming presence of God calls him to become a leader for his people. Through Moses, God summons the Israelites to leave their slavery behind them and to set out on a new journey. Once again the spirit of God moves across the waters, this time to create a way to freedom. "Yahweh drove back the sea with a strong easterly wind all night, and he made dry land of the sea" (Ex 14:21). The slaves walk through the chaos—their own and that of the dark waters surrounding them—and they emerge reborn. They are "baptized," they are plunged into the dark waters. When they emerge their slavery is behind them. A new life awaits them. In the sea journey and in the desert sun they are re-created into a people of freedom, a people chosen, shaped, and loved into life by Yahweh. Creation continues as liberation. The helplessness of human life is transformed into power and action.

The prophets develop this creative pattern in new directions. In their lives and in their preaching the wind and the fire are experienced as an inward presence. The wind is interiorized into the breath of love and the call to inner renewal. The fire is experienced as the burning call to preach the Word of God. Isaiah responds to this call by crying out for the purifying flame. Ezechiel promises new breath for the dry, dead bones of an exiled people. Joel foretells an age when the spirit of God will be poured out on all people. Finally, in the writings of Deutero-Isaiah, the prophetic vision centers on the mysterious figure of the suffering servant of Yahweh. He will receive the spirit of God for a mission of healing and liberation. "The spirit of the Lord Yahweh has been given to me. He has sent me to bring good news to the poor, to bind up hearts that are broken, to proclaim liberty to captives, freedom to those in prison, to proclaim a year of favor from Yahweh . . ." (Is 61:1-2).

These are the words that Jesus claims for himself at the beginning of his public ministry. Jesus is the fulfillment of the pattern of creativity and purification. He is the enfleshment of God's spirit. He is the wind and the fire of the Father.

By his own description, John the Baptist came to prepare, not to fulfill. He waited for the definitive breakthrough of God's spirit in the world. He scanned the horizon of human life in search of the wind and the fire of a new creation. "I baptize you with water," he tells the crowds, "but someone is coming, someone who is more powerful than I am, and I am not fit to undo the strap of his sandals; he will baptize you with the Holy Spirit and with fire" (Lk 3:16).

Jesus is the beginning of the new creation. He is the way in which God moves across the chaos of human existence to create a new heaven and a new earth. In him the Father chooses a new people for himself.

Before Jesus inaugurates the new creation he experiences the breath and flame of the Spirit in his own life. The Spirit hovers over him in the waters of the Jordan. The language and images which the evangelists employ to describe the baptism of Jesus clearly echo the opening words of Genesis. Jesus emerges from the water with a deeper awareness that he is loved by the Father. He experiences the presence of the Spirit within him. Like his ancestors, Jesus is led into the desert by the Spirit. There the creative breath shapes his inner self. The purifying flame prepares him for his final passover.

As Jesus draws near to his suffering and death, he shares the experience of the Spirit within him. He tells his disciples of his longing to communicate this creative and purifying presence to others. "I have come to bring fire to the earth, and how I wish it were blazing already! There is a baptism I must still receive, and how great is my distress till it is over" (Lk 12:49-50)!

The hour of Jesus arrives. He embraces his "baptism"—the plunging, dark journey of the cross and the triumph of the resurrection. With an anguished cry he "hands over the Spirit." This phrase refers not only to the death of Jesus, but also to the manner in which he communicates the Spirit to a new humanity. The spirit of Jesus, the *breath* of Jesus, is the Holy Spirit. On the cross Jesus brings fire to the earth. He sets it ablaze with love.

After his resurrection, Jesus returns to the upper room where his disciples are hiding. Their world has fallen apart. Confused and fearful, they find themselves surrounded by chaos. Jesus breaks through their walls. He breaks down the doors of fear. He stands before them and *breathes* on them: "Receive the Holy Spirit . . ." (Jn 20:22). As Yahweh breathed into the clay of Adam; as Ezechiel promised that God would breathe into the dead bones of Israel; so Jesus breathes his Spirit into a new humanity.

On Pentecost this new humanity is born. The wind and the fire of God burst into the hearts of the disciples. They are transformed into new people. "When Pentecost day came round, they had all met in one room when suddenly they heard what sounded like a powerful wind from heaven, the noise of which filled the entire house in which they were sitting; and something appeared to them that seemed like tongues of fire; these separated and came to rest on the head of each of them. They were all filled with the Holy Spirit . . ." (Ac 2:1-4).

The wind and the fire. Creativity and purification. This is the continuing pattern with which God leads his creation toward fulfillment. In Jesus this pattern is an inward journey rather than an outward force. It is the journey which is realized in every Christian who seeks for the fullness of life by living the paschal mystery.

What does this pattern mean for us? How can we relate the meaning of this creative and purifying journey to our lives? In what sense does Jesus continue to baptize us with the Holy Spirit and with fire?

First, the Spirit comes into our lives to create. Birth is not an isolated moment, it is a life process. Our growth toward wholeness is a gradual unfolding that involves conflict and struggle. Like the world around us we grow and change. We are being born each day. St. Paul compares the growth of our inner selves to the evolution of creation. "From the beginning until now, the entire creation as we know has been groaning in one great act of giving birth; and not only creation but all of us who possess the first fruits of the spirit, we, too, groan inwardly as we wait for our bodies to be set free" (Rm 8:22-23).

At birth our lives resemble the dark waters before creation. We are a wilderness, an abyss that waits to be shaped and formed by the Spirit. We come into the world under the sentence of Cain. We

bear the mark of violence. We live east of Eden. We
are wanderers across the face of the earth.

God calls us out of chaos into community. Re-
demption is simply another word for re-creation
through the Spirit. He penetrates our wilderness to
create what Isaiah calls "the sacred way."

At first, God's creative power can appear to be a
destructive force, a terrifying energy. The Christian exodus from slavery to freedom reveals that
there can be no rebirth without dying. There cannot
be new life without the pangs of birth. The journey
of faith is a midnight wrestling with the Spirit.
Before he can give us his gifts of patience and peace,
he enters our lives as wind and fire. We must encounter God as a creative force before we know him
as a quiet presence. Gerard Manley Hopkins describes this experience in the opening lines of *The
Wreck of the Deutschland:*

> Thou mastering me
>   God! giver of breath and bread;
> World's strand, sway of the sea;
>   Lord of living and dead;
> Thou hast bound bones and veins in me, fastened me flesh,
> And after it almost unmade, what with dread,
>   Thy doing: and dost thou touch me afresh?
> Over again I feel thy finger and find thee.[2]

Contemporary moral theologians sometimes speak
of the emergence of a "fundamental option" in our

lives. What do they mean by this? Among other things, they are speaking of the confrontation between the Spirit and our inner selves. They are describing the arduous process of clarifying our values and of interiorizing our convictions. The sacred way that leads toward personal vision is sometimes long and lonely. Each day we are being created. Each day we are participating in our own creation.

Secondly the Spirit comes into our lives to purify. Creativity demands purification. Besides the wind, there is the fire. Before God can fill us with his life, he must cleanse us with his fire.

The process of purification is often misinterpreted as a negation of life. This misunderstanding has given rise to a theology of asceticism which separates our daily experience from our eternal destiny. Essentially, purification is a more intense form of creation. It is the energy of the Spirit leading us toward fulfillment.

Life provides its own purifiers. The daily struggle for growth refines that which is real. It liberates the energy of life that waits beneath the surface of our life. "And now I have put you in the fire like silver," Yahweh says to his people. "I have tested you in the furnace of distress" (Is 48:10). For the authentic to emerge, that which is inauthentic must be burned away. The great mystics describe this experience as "the dark night of the senses." Like purification, the dark night has frequently been misunderstood. It has been interpreted as the attempt to root out or suppress our human feelings. In reality, the dark night of the senses is the painful side of growth. It is the honing and the deepening of our emotions. It is the refining of our feelings to make them sensitive to life and responsive to beauty. It is growth toward heightened awareness. It is the journey toward emotional integration. Understood in this way, mortification takes on a creative dimension. Self-discipline is not intended to destroy our desire but to direct it toward life. "Like blind men we grope in a world of textures, afraid to touch the jagged edges of life. But the man who reaches out to embrace them finds that those same edges that have pierced him have also made him whole."[3]

In the gospel, Jesus tells his disciples that they must be "salted with fire" (Mk 9:48). Salt enhances the flavor of food. Fire strengthens the quality of metal. Jesus is saying that purification is intended to bring out the best in our lives.

There are not two different sources of life in us. There are not two different fires. There is one flame—the flame of the Spirit permeating our lives. Our desire for beauty is not, in the end, different from our desire to be united forever with God. The fire of the Spirit integrates our desires and transforms them into a longing for eternal life.

God continues to speak to us in the midst of this purifying struggle. It is as though we ourselves are the burning bush in which we encounter the living God. We are purified but not consumed. We are seared but not destroyed. God speaks to us in the depths of our hearts. He is present in the painful process of growth. He reveals his name as the source of life and as the promise of fulfillment. In the experience of purification we become holy ground. We are invited to take off our shoes and walk barefoot into life.

Finally, the Spirit invites us to integrate our lives. The wind and the fire of God create order out of chaos. They separate the authentic from the inauthentic. To complete the creative work, the wind and the fire unify the elements of creation into a design of harmony and beauty. This unifying experience in our lives is the discovery of our own truth. It is the Spirit's way of leading us to the gifts that are uniquely our own.

Jeremiah pictures God as a potter who shapes his people with loving care (cf Jer 18:1f). Like a potter who centers the clay on his wheel, the Spirit centers our lives through his creative energy. The Spirit puts us in touch with our true selves. He enables us to pierce through the superficial masks and roles to discover our still point.

In the Christian tradition there is a word we use to describe this growth toward integration. The word is "holiness." "Be holy, for I, Yahweh Your God, am holy" (Lv 19:2). In the Old Testament, holiness had a specific and somewhat limited meaning. It referred to those persons or objects which were set apart from the everyday and consecrated to God. Holiness implies separation from ordinary life. The priests, the temple and its furnishings were considered sacred. They were looked upon as holy in contrast to the rest of life which was profane.

In the New Testament this notion of holiness undergoes a radical change. Jesus is the holiness of the Father become flesh. He is the source of life made present in the everyday. Jesus breaks through the veil of the temple. He unites human life and divine presence. The Christian community is the living temple of the Spirit. Because of Jesus, all life is sacred. Holiness does not separate us from life. It is a quality of all experience. Holiness is the wholeness that comes from the creative and purifying presence of the Spirit. For a Christian, the search for wholeness parallels the growth toward holiness.

In the New Testament, Jesus substitutes the word "perfect" for holy. "You must therefore be perfect just as your heavenly Father is perfect" (Mt 5:48), he tells his followers. When Jesus speaks of perfection he is not referring to our attitude toward law. Perfection is another word for wholeness. It is not a goal that we achieve by ourselves; it is a process which the Spirit accomplishes in us.

There is an ancient myth about the god Prometheus who stole fire from the gods and brought it to mankind. He was subsequently punished by the other gods because he had given a power to mortals which they could use to their advantage.

Jesus brings fire to the earth. But he brings a different kind of fire, and he gives it in a different way. Unlike Prometheus, Jesus has not stolen the fire. He received it as a gift from the Father. The fire which Jesus brings to earth is the fire of love, the Holy Spirit. We receive this gift when we open our lives in faith. For a Christian, fulfillment is not a prize that is won. It is not a flame that is stolen from the gods. It is a gift which is received from the Source of all creativity and life.

This fire is the promise of fulfillment which Christianity offers to the world. This is the fire which Jesus has set ablaze in our hearts. "The day will come," writes Teilhard, "when, after harnessing space, the winds, the tides, gravitation, we shall harness for God the energies of love. And, on that day, for the second time in the history of the world, man will have discovered fire."[4]

FOOTNOTES

1. *Jerusalem Bible* (London: Darton, Longman, & Todd, Ltd.; and New York: Doubleday and Co. Inc., 1966), p. 15, cf. footnote "b".
2. Hopkins, "The Wreck of the Deutschland" in *Poems and Prose*, p. 12.
3. Author Unknown.
4. Teilhard de Chardin, *Toward the Future* (New York: Harcourt Brace Jovanovich, 1975), p. 86.

Chapter Six

By This Will All Men Know

THE BOND OF LOVE

It was late when the doorbell rang. I went downstairs with the feeling of uneasiness that accompanies an unexpected call at night. In the doorway, framed in darkness, was a young woman with light hair, a brightly colored dress, and bare feet. She was crying.

"I need to talk to someone," she said simply.

Inside, in the light, I could see that she was even younger than she had appeared in the darkness. She began to speak quietly, fighting back tears.

"My name is Sandy. I'm fourteen years old."

Slowly, she shared her story. Two nights ago her older brother had been murdered. Tonight, at the funeral home, a feeling of aloneness and fear came over Sandy. As she watched relatives and friends file past the coffin, the awful truth touched her. Her brother was dead. He would never come home again.

I could see the question "Why?" forming in her eyes. A familiar feeling of helplessness moved inside of me.

"What are you feeling now, Sandy?" I asked her.

"I feel like I want to be alone forever. But the feeling frightens me. That's why I thought I should talk to someone."

For some time we were both silent. Then Sandy shared more of her sense of loss and her search for meaning. After we had talked at some length, I took her home.

When I returned, I couldn't sleep. For some reason I was haunted by Sandy's initial statement. *I feel like I want to be alone forever. But the feeling frightens me. . . .*

What was Sandy really saying? What was she afraid of? Why did her words leave me with only silence? I had the feeling that Sandy had said something which neither of us fully understood.

Sometime during the tossing and turning of that night, the deeper meaning of Sandy's statement became clearer to me. In a moment of anguish, she had given words to two of our deepest fears: The fear of closeness and the fear of loneliness. The fear of what love demands of us and the fear of losing love forever. The fear of risking openness with another and the fear of the isolation which results if we never take the risk. Which is more painful, Sandy seemed to be asking, to choose love and risk losing closeness, or to choose not to love at all?

Sandy expressed a feeling that moves through the

waking and sleeping hours of many people today. At
a time of painful separation, our first instinct, like
Sandy's, is to feel that it's not worth it. Loving is too
painful. We never know when we will lose the
person we love. We never know when a relationship
will end. Perhaps it is easier not to get involved. *I
feel like I want to be alone forever. . . .*

But the feeling frightens me. . . . While the fear of
loss is deep in us, there is an even stronger fear. It
is the fear that we may actually be alone forever.
What if there were no one who would break through
the walls of our loneliness and share our lives with
us? What if we were to be alone forever? We want
there to be someone who will overcome our isolation, someone who will never leave us. We reach out
for lasting communion.

There are some people today who seem, by their
way of life, to be saying, "I want to be alone forever." They represent the new age of individualism.
They invest more time and energy in the pursuit of
success than in the pursuit of friendship. They seek
to live the good life without the responsibility of
permanent ties. They are the loners who have been
hurt by relationships that haven't worked out. They
have decided that involvement is too costly.

There is a growing disillusionment with superficial relationships. The divorce rate continues to
climb, especially in young marriages. The genera-

tion gap still haunts many families. Many of the communes which began in a spirit of optimism have dissolved in a feeling of bitterness. "We just don't speak the same language." "We're just not in the same place." How often we hear these phrases or use them ourselves.

There is also a new realism in the way we portray human relationships. Writers and other artists are exploring the lack of communication that takes place between people. Many films expose the blindness and manipulation that occur behind the outward gestures of love. For more than two decades Ingmar Bergman has portrayed the inability of persons to share a world of common experience. His films explore the failure to find ways of bridging the infinite space between people. The age of romantic love is gone. Gone, too, is the happy ending. Human relationships have been unmasked. D. H. Lawrence describes love as though it were an irresistible, biological force which destroys communion as often as it creates it. Freud and other psychologists speak of the hidden forms of aggression sometimes present in sexuality.

This realism is healthy and, in its own way, liberating. A sense of reality gives us firm ground on which to walk. It gives us goals that relate to daily experience. But authentic realism retains a spirit of hopefulness. In our age realism often gives way to a cynicism that dismisses the possibility of lasting relationships. All around us, like gutted buildings in the inner city, we find the remains of community, the ruins of love. We are surrounded by brokenness.

Ironically, this cynical attitude toward love is growing at the very time that the technology of communication is making its greatest leap forward in history. We have telstar and hot lines. We have computers with instant information. We can view a football play from seven different angles, but often we cannot see or hear the person who is next to us.

The disillusioned feel that love costs too much. It is simpler to walk alone. It is too painful to risk the kind of vulnerability that comes in an intimate and lasting relationship.

The result of this cynicism is a growing trend toward the private world of fulfillment. This is the age of the loner. It is the time of careers and professions and the independent life. The quest for self-fulfillment becomes a full-time occupation—my job, my future, my meaning, my world. Relationships are kept on a passing and casual level. They are functional. They are not to interfere. Many people have grown weary of the pain that comes from relationships that do not last. They are weary of feeling used or owned or manipulated. They want to be free. "Hell," writes Jean Paul Sartre, "is other people." *I feel like I want to be alone forever.* . . .

But the feeling frightens me. Even as we cringe at the cost of love, we instinctively reach out for companionship. In the end, the desire to share is stronger than the impulse to run. The longing to break down the walls of loneliness is greater than the fear of losing the gift of love. The yearning to be completed by the presence of another person is the deepest of all human hungers. When we are growing up, we wonder if there will ever be someone who will see what we see, hear what we hear, and feel what we feel. We wonder if our inner world will ever be a shared world. According to Gabriel Marcel, a contemporary of Sartre's, the deepest human fear is the fear of eternal isolation. "There is only one suffering," writes Marcel, "that is, to be alone."

Despite the growing cynicism regarding relationships, the search to overcome our loneliness persists. We are born to live in friendship, and even as we flee from it in fear, we reach out for it in longing. The contemporary unmasking of love only reveals the aching heart of our loneliness. The search for community continues. In families, in groups of friends, in religious communities and in parishes, the search for a shared life persists. The initial enthusiasm regarding communes seems to have ended, but the serious groups have continued. Most of these are based on religious values that place high priority on a shared style of life.

"In love there can be no fear," writes St. John, "but fear is driven out by perfect love" (I Jn 4:18). Like Sandy, like all of us, Christianity looks at love from both sides. It knows the ambiguity of the human heart which at once fears and wants love. It knows the fear of intimacy as well as the dread of loneliness. But Christianity locates this tension in a different setting. In the gospel, the double side of love is seen in terms of death and resurrection. A Christian experiences the fear of closeness and the dread of loneliness as a call to die to self. The tension is an invitation to let go of the desire for security and to risk pain for the sake of communion. In the gospel, it is not "love's illusion we recall," but the *gift* of love and the *cost* of love which are transformed into the *triumph* of love.

Christians believe that fulfillment is not a private pursuit but a shared gift. They choose to face the darkness of relationships without becoming cynical. They commit themselves to love's possibilities without becoming sentimental. The Christian way to fulfillment confronts the brokenness of human life. It seeks to heal that brokenness with the gift of the Father's love. Christianity begins with the assumption that, of ourselves, we cannot love each other consistently and faithfully. This is why we need to be redeemed and healed. "This is the love I mean: Not our love for God, but God's love for us when he sent his Son to be the sacrifice that takes away our sins" (I Jn 4:10).

In a world which looks with cynicism on love and its implications, the life of faith still summons us to share community. In the midst of the ruins there are signs of hope. There are small groups of Christians who are continuing to seek out the bonds of love at the heart of their lives. They are neither cynical nor romantic. They are simply struggling to be faithful disciples of the risen Lord.

What are these bonds of love for a Christian? How is the gospel a way that leads to fulfillment in communion with others? Why do people care for one another? What is the basis for community?

At one time, need—the practical need of survival was the primary reason for community. Early tribes stayed together because they shared the same blood, and blood was looked upon as life itself. The survival of the community was provided for through children. The members of a tribe cared for one another out of a desire for self-protection and continuity. The basis of relationships was survival.

There were other considerations also. Until modern times, some of the reasons for marriage were economic. The story of *Fiddler on the Roof* is an account of the tension which occurs when love, rather than economics, becomes the reason for marriage. Tevye, the father in *Fiddler on the Roof*, is a likeable man with many difficulties. He is a member of an ethnic minority. He is poor. There are rumors of persecutions. But his most pressing problem has to do with his own daughters. Tevye must face a revolution in his own family. One by one, his daughters decide to marry for reasons of love rather than economic security.

To be in relation to another person for the sake of love transforms the meaning of marriage. It moves it from function to friendship, from economics to grace. The Christian gospel challenges us to locate the meaning of relationships in the experience of love.

This transformation began early in the Judeo-Christian tradition. In describing the nature of sexuality, Genesis speaks of it in the context of loving companionship rather than as a biological function. "It is not good that the man should be alone. I will make him a helpmate" (Gn 2:18). Sharing life is the essential purpose of human relationships. Love overcomes the loneliness with which we are born.

The economic and social reasons for love continued to play a major role in the Old Testament. Despite the growing personal emphasis in the *Song of Songs* and the *Book of Ruth*, the tribal and economic emphasis persisted. It mattered what tribe you belonged to. It made a difference whether you were a man or a woman. It mattered what social or economic class you were in.

In his life and teaching, Jesus brings about a decisive revolution in the understanding of love. This is apparent, first of all, in Jesus' own experience of community. He is not a loner. The first act of his public ministry is to begin forming a small community. Jesus is part of a tradition of itinerant rabbis who gather followers as they move along the roads of Galilee. Yet, even in this, Jesus is different. Jesus seeks to form more than an intellectual relationship with his disciples. He is more than a teacher. He invites them to enter a personal relationship based on commitment to one another. He reverses the roles of master and servant, teacher and student. He tells his followers that the great ones must serve the lesser. He washes their feet. He stands in their midst as one who serves.

Jesus reaches out beyond his immediate community. He changes the boundaries of love. It is significant that Jesus is condemned for the company he keeps. He identifies his life with the poor and the outcast. He breaks through the established social and religious laws for relationships. It is ritually unclean to touch lepers or to associate with foreigners. It is socially unacceptable for a man to talk with a woman, especially a Samaritan woman, in public. It is considered a religious taboo to reach out to tax collectors and sinners.

In his style of relating, Jesus creates a new basis for human community. He pierces beneath the social roles and searches for the deeper bond that unites human persons. He even goes beyond those bonds which are most dear to his people—the bonds of marriage and family.

There is a scene in the gospel which illustrates this revolution in relationships. The crowds are pressing around Jesus, listening to his teaching. Word is sent to Jesus that his mother and his relatives are waiting outside and want to see him. For a Jew, family needs are primary. Jesus pauses for a moment and studies the faces of the people who surround him. Then he replies, "Who is my mother? Who are my brothers?" He stretches out his hands toward those around him and says, "Here are my mother and my brothers. Anyone who does the will of my Father in heaven, he is my brother and sister and mother" (Mt 12:46-50).

For Jesus, the basis for human relationships transcends all social or biological roles. Love goes beyond culture and economics. There is a bond which is deeper than tribal ties, deeper than family loyalty, deeper even than the love between husband and wife.

At the last supper, Jesus reveals the nature of this deeper bond of love. He tells his disciples, "I shall not call you servants anymore, because a servant does not know his master's business; I call you friends because I have made known to you everything I have learnt from my Father. . . . I give you a new commandment: Love one another; just as I have loved you, you also must love one another. By this love you have for one another, everyone will know that you are my disciples" (Jn 15:15; 13: 34-35).

These words are all the more significant because of the setting in which Jesus spoke them. It is his last meal with his disciples. It is the passover, the feast of freedom and solidarity. Aware of what lies ahead of him, Jesus shares his deepest feelings about the meaning of love. He is not just urging his followers to care for one another. He is giving them a new basis for human relationships. He is establishing a new bond of love. I call you *friends*. Friendship is the model for all human communion. Friendship is the fulfillment of our longing to share life.

What, in turn, is the basis for friendship: What is the experience from which Jesus draws his understanding of friendship as central to human life?

The answer to these questions can be found in the nature of Jesus' relationship with his Father. Jesus understands human love in the light of the communion which he shares with the Father. No other religion reveals such an intimate union of persons.

In reading the gospels we can see the ways in which this relationship between Jesus and the Father deepened and grew. The baptism in the Jordan was a turning point in Jesus' awareness of the Father's love for him. "This is my Son, the Beloved; my favor rests on him" (Mt 3:17). During the long nights of prayer in the wilderness and in "the lonely places," Jesus' relationship with his Father developed beyond nearness to intimacy, and beyond intimacy to union. At the last supper, Jesus tells his disciples, "To have seen me is to have seen the Father, so how can you say, 'Let us see the Father?' Do you not believe that I am in the Father and the Father is in me? The words I say to you I do not speak as from myself: It is the Father, living in me, who is doing this work" (Jn 14:9-10).

Jesus invites others to share his relationship with the Father. "If anyone loves me he will keep my word, and my Father will love him, and we shall come and make our home with him" (Jn 14:23). Be cause of the depth of love which he has experience Jesus sees infinite possibilities for human co munity. Human relationships must be modeled the bond between Jesus and the Father. Thus, Christian ethic moves beyond the golden r There is more to loving others than simply trea

them as you would have them treat you. It is not
just a case of "getting along" with others. It is not
enough to be "nice" to them. Jesus demands more.
"Love one another as I have loved you. A man can
have no greater love than to lay down his life for his
friends . . ." (Jn 15:13).

It is this radical experience of love which Jesus
designates as *the* sign of his new community. "By
this love you have for one another, everyone will
know that you are my disciples" (Jn 13:35).

There remains a further dimension in the Christian call to love. It involves the relationship of love
to eternal life. In the gospels, eternal life is another
word for fulfillment. When Jesus speaks of eternal
life, he is not describing how long we will exist after
we die. He is not referring to the Greek notion of
immortality. Eternal life is an inward experience
that begins with faith and grows in love. It is a
quality of human life, rather than the quantitative
measurement of its survival. Eternal life is like a
seed which grows, buds, and finally blossoms into
fullness. "Eternal life is this: to know you, the only
true God, and Jesus Christ who you have sent" (Jn
17:3). In other words, eternal life is essentially a
relationship. The specific nature of this relationship
is that of *knowing*. Ordinarily, when we use the
term, to know, we refer to our understanding of
certain facts. When scripture uses the term, it

means something different. For the Hebrew, knowledge is personal and experiential. It implies more than the intellectual grasp of certain facts *about* someone. Rather, it connotes a total and immediate experience of a person. To know is to share intimately.

For Jesus, eternal life is the communion which he experiences with the Father and which he seeks to communicate to his followers. "I shall not call you servants any more, because a servant does not *know* his master's business. I call you friends because I have made *known* to you everything I have learnt from my Father."

Friendship is related to this biblical experience of *knowing*. It only becomes a reality when we share ourselves with others. Just as the Father reveals his inner life to Jesus, so Jesus, through the gift of his Spirit, communicates his inner self to us. We, too, grow in friendship only to the extent that we share what is within us.

The scriptural notion of self-revelation implies more than instant intimacy. The communion to which Jesus calls us is deeper and more demanding than simply sharing our feelings. Love begins in self-revelation, but it grows in the slow, patient sharing of our struggle and pain, our values and our search. Jesus tells his friends that the most important gift he can share with them is his experience of

the Father. The same is true for us. The deepest
sign of human intimacy is to share the search for
God. We share that experience not only when we
pray with others, but also when we struggle with
the mystery of friendship.

Love is neither easy nor comfortable. Christian
friendship demands a laying down of our lives, a
dying to self daily. It demands that we surrender
our grasp on false security. It asks of us a willingness to become vulnerable. Christian love is not a
sentimental dream. It is as real as the road to Jerusalem. Sometimes it is as lonely as the night in
Gethsemane. Only those who share their fears and
pain, as well as their affection and joy, have touched
the mystery of Christian love. "Love in action,"
writes Dostoevsky, "is a harsh and dreadful thing
compared to love in dreams."[1]

The journey of Christian friendship is long. The
fullness of its joy can only be measured by the price
of its growth. There are times when we feel aban-
doned and alone. There are times when those
closest to us cannot watch with us. There are times
when they do not understand. These are the most
painful moments of all, for they involve us in the
dark side of the human condition. Jesus experienced
this loneliness with his own disciples. "Have I been
with you all this time, Philip, and you still do not
know me" (Jn 14:9)?

Like Jesus, we cannot experience the supportive presence of love if we are not willing to walk with its darkness and, sometimes, with its failure. The great mystics describe the struggle to grow toward union with God as "the dark night of the soul." In our lives the search to find union with God cannot be separated from our efforts to discover communion with others. In a sense, every friendship draws us into the dark night of the soul. It is the struggle to share life deeply and honestly. It is the pain that accompanies our attempts to accept our own helplessness and to love the darkness which we encounter in our friends.

Ultimately, the strength of Christian love is rooted in God's love for us. We can risk entering the fearful, joyful struggle of friendship because we trust in God's faithful love. In the end, "nothing can separate us from the love of Christ . . . neither death nor life, no angel, no prince, nothing that exists, nothing still to come, not any power, or height or depth, nor any created thing, can ever come between us and the love of God made visible in Christ Jesus our Lord" (Rm 8:35, 38-39).

FOOTNOTES

1. The words of Father Zossima in *The Brothers Kara-mazov*. This is a favorite quotation of Dorothy Day. It is part of the title of a biographical account of her life and the Catholic Worker Movement: William D. Miller, *A Harsh and Dreadful Love* (New York: Doubleday Image Books, 1974). I am indebted to this source for the reference.

Chapter Seven

It is Finished

THE FULFILLMENT OF LIFE

In Nikos Kazantzakis' novel, *Zorba the Greek*, there is a scene in which Zorba asks his young friend:

> ". . . 'Why do people die?'
> 'I don't know,' I replied, ashamed, as if I had been asked the simplest thing, the most essential thing, and was unable to explain it.
> 'You don't know!' said Zorba in round-eyed astonishment. . . . Well, all those damned books you read—what good are they? If they don't tell you that, what do they tell you?'
> 'They tell me about the perplexity of mankind, who can give no answer to the question you've just put me.'"[1]

Death is the troubled question that enters the horizon of every human life. As no other experience in our lives, death seems to block the way to fulfillment. All the books in the world have not been able to fathom its dark meaning. Despite the centuries of intellectual probing and the attempts to understand

111

the why of death, we have no satisfying answers. We have only a long history of questions like Zorba's and an even longer history of human perplexity. Yet, if we are to view life as ultimately fulfilling, death must not only be questioned, it must be confronted. The Christian vision depends on our understanding of death as a way to new life.

Christianity does not offer a solution to death. It simply gives us the person of Jesus who experienced death and moved through its dark waters to new life. For Christians, death is not an intellectual puzzle. It is an experience, a passover, a journey. The wrestling of Christianity with death is not in the realm of speculation. It is in the world of living and dying. Christians do not try to find answers for death. They look for a way of transforming the experience of dying. The gospel tells us that death is a doorway, not a dead end. The good news of Christianity is that death can be the way to the fullness of life.

The German philosopher, Martin Heidegger, claims that we cannot imagine our own death. We hear of the death of a close friend and we weep. We stand at the bedside of our parents in their last moments of life. We share their last agony with the intense awareness that part of our own life will die with them. Although there is something we can share with those who die, our involvement is limited and fragmentary. However close we are to a dying person, there is a distance that we cannot bridge, a chasm that we cannot cross. In the end, we can only stand by, compassionately but helplessly. We can only offer the presence of our lives to those who are dying. Death, like life, is something that we cannot learn about vicariously. We must experience it in order to understand it.

My death remains beyond my experience and my ability to imagine. According to Dr. Elisabeth Kübler Ross, there is an instinctive tendency to deny one's own death. I would like to think that I will live forever. Death is an experience that happens to others but not to me. Mortality remains an abstraction, a comfortable generality. All humanity is mortal. But I am not humanity, and I am alive.

At some point I will experience the approach of my death. In that hour it will no longer be an abstraction. I will experience it as an urgent reality about to impose itself on my life. I will be faced with the inevitable: I am going to die . . . *now*, not later on, not thirty years from now, or next month, not tomorrow, but this moment my life is about to end.

What will my concerns be when I confront death? What will be uppermost in my mind?

We might expect that our thoughts will be about the afterlife. However, the experience of those who have come close to death, and the experience of

those who have reflected on the meaning of dying
reveals something different. Death is the climax of
life. It is the testing ground of life's value. The primary focus of that moment is not the afterlife but
the significance of these days and years that have
been our earthly existence. Death is a time of decision about life, a time when we stand at the cross-
roads. Regardless of what we believe about the
afterlife, we must choose what we think about this
life.

What did it mean to walk the earth? What were
the days of my life about? The eating and sleeping?
The sunsets and the dreams? The tears and the
laughter? The fears, the aches and the hunger?

Throughout his public ministry Jesus often spoke
of the hour of his death. The final words and feelings
of Jesus tell us something of the way he approached
his death. They tell us of his concerns at that time.
In what sense did he experience his death as the fulfillment of life? What can we learn from him about
the meaning of our own death?

The gospel of St. John describes Jesus' death
with these words: "After this, aware that all was
finished, in order to bring scripture to its complete
fulfillment, Jesus said: 'I am thirsty.' There was at
hand a jar full of common wine so they stuck a
sponge soaked in wine on some hyssop and raised it

to his lips. When Jesus took the wine, he exclaimed:
'It is finished' and bowing his head, he handed over
the Spirit" (Jn 19:28-30).[2]

I am thirsty.

It is finished.

These are the last words of Jesus. They are a
summary of his human experience. They describe
the meaning he found in his existence: Thirsting for
life and seeking to realize it through love. Thirst and
fullness. Yearning and completion. In the beginning
is the hunger, the thirst, the longing. In the end is
the fullness, the completion, the consummation.
These are not separate experiences for Jesus. Even
as they come together at the end of his life, so they
were always present in him. The longing for life and
the fullness of its mystery were part of Jesus' daily
experience and growth. There is a fullness of
promise at the beginning. There is a thirst for life to
the end.

I am thirsty. At the moment of death, Jesus'
whole self fills with a final longing for life.

I am thirsty. It is a cry of yearning for the beauty
of creation which he has known and the companionship which he has shared. It is a cry of yearning for
the fullness of life, which he experienced in his relationship with his Father. It is a cry of longing that
has permeated his life and his teaching. . . .

"I am thirsty," he said to the woman at the well of Jacob. Then he shared with her a deeper thirst for living water.

"I have longed to eat this passover with you before I suffer," he says to his friends at their last meal "because I tell you, I shall not eat it again until it is fulfilled in the kingdom of God" (Lk 22:15-16).

I am thirsty. Jesus speaks for every human heart. He expresses our longing to overcome all division and brokenness. He speaks for the lonely and the searching who have no voice. He gathers together all the yearning of those who have ever been born. I am thirsty, he cries, and the world finds meaning and voice for its longing.

It is finished. In Jesus' final thirst, there is an experience of completion. Something immense and powerful is moving toward fulfillment.

It is finished. What does Jesus mean? These could be the words of any person who faces death. And for every person, they could have a different meaning.

It is finished. Some people say these words with regret, even despair. As death approaches they look backward in bitterness. They feel that "it is all over." Life is ended. It is cut off like a blade of grass. It is finished like a song that once was and is no more, like a day that sinks into eternal night.

It is finished. Others say these words with a sense of relief. *Finally*, it is over. Life is a road of pain, an experience of absurdity. It is a time of delusion, with eyes that do not meet and voices that do not speak. Now, at last, it is ended. These people greet death as liberation, as an escape from an impossible situation.

It is finished. What did Jesus mean when he said these words? He loved life too intensely to find it absurd. It was not easy for him to face death or to leave the beauty of the earth and the companionship of his friends. In the garden, he experienced dread in the face of death. It was difficult for him to die. But it was not a feeling of regret that Jesus expressed at the moment of his death.

In his agony, Jesus also longs for release and for total peace. He pleads for the cup to pass him by. But as he faces death, relief is not the primary feeling that Jesus experiences.

It is finished. This is a cry of *victory.* These words flow from an experience of the fullness of life. Jesus is saying that his work is accomplished, it is consummated, it is fulfilled. Everything comes together in this moment. Jesus gathers up his entire life and freely gives it to the Father. He does this, not with regret nor with a sense of relief, but with love and trust. His life is fulfilled.

"My Father goes on working and so do I" (Jn 5:17). He had once spoken these words to those who did not understand his mission, Now, it is finished.

His work is done. The hour has come. In his death, Jesus finds the fulfillment of his life.

How can this be true? How can that which seems to extinguish life, to limit it, even destroy it, be experienced as fulfillment?

We often look to the resurrection to answer this question. Death is an experience of fullness, we say, because Jesus rose again. He overcame death by breaking out of the tomb. This is true. The resurrection is the final triumph and breakthrough of Jesus to fulfillment. However, we can too easily look to the afterlife to answer the enigma of death. To look upon the resurrection as a narrow escape from death is to miss the full meaning of human life. It is to miss the death and resurrection that is present in every moment. It is a failure to see the value and beauty of human experience as a journey toward fulfillment.

Death and resurrection are not separate from life. They do more than tell us where we are going; they tell us who we are. They are not just future; they are present. In order to understand the biblical significance of death as the fulfillment of life, we must reflect on the dying and the rising in daily life. The kingdom of God is unfolding within us. The real question for a Christian is not whether there is life after death but whether there is life after birth. Is there life emerging from the dying and rising of each day?

The temptation exists to push death and resurrection out of human life. We see death and resurrection as ultimate events rather than as immediate experiences. This is not the way in which Jesus speaks of them: "Unless you take up your cross daily and follow me, you will not have eternal life." Death and life are not abstractions or final events; they are daily choices. "See, *today* I set before you life and prosperity, death and disaster . . . choose life then so that you and your descendants may live . . ." (Dt 30:15, 19).

Christianity is a religion of life. It is an invitation to choose life in all of the circumstances in which we find ourselves. If it is an invitation to choose life, it is also a call to confront death. Death is not the termination of life; it is the struggle at the center of life. It is the rhythm of agony and ecstasy as we move from yearning at birth to fulfillment at death. It is the journey, the inner exodus from the old self to the new. "I die daily," says St. Paul.

There is an ancient proverb which says "as soon as we are born, we are old enough to die." Ordinarily, this is understood as a commentary on the fragility of human life. For a Christian, this proverb has positive significance. Its meaning is found in the gospels, in the paradoxical words of Jesus: "He who would save his life must lose it. He who gives up his life for my sake and for the sake of the gospel will find it." To choose life daily is to encounter the mystery of dying to self in love, in work, in commitment, and in life decisions. As Christians, we can put the proverb in another way: "As soon as we die to self, we are young enough to live."

Perhaps Heidegger is right. We cannot imagine our own death. In the last analysis, this is not what matters. What matters is that we live our lives, that we transform our daily dying with freely chosen love. The urgency of the final hour is contained in the unfolding of daily life.

Not long ago most people were born and died at home. Many grew up hearing the cry of a newborn baby. They stood by their grandmother's bed when she died. Now, babies are born in maternity wards and grandmothers die in rest homes. In this process, we have lost something. We have lost the sense that birth and death are a part of the rhythm of life.

I became aware of this when I had my first encounter with death. I learned something about my life when I stood at the bedside of a man who was dying.

He was old. I had never met him before. I waited at his side, in the quiet of his hospital room, as he came to grips with death. I still remember his name. I recall feeling a sense of awe as I shared the experience of death with someone with whom I had shared nothing of life. Yet, in those last moments, even though he was unable to speak, he told me about his life and about life everywhere. Just before he died, there was a visible struggle. He had been quiet for some time. His breathing was slow, almost imperceptible. Then, suddenly, he began to struggle and to gasp for breath. He opened his eyes. I sensed terror and fear in him. His struggle continued. His fear seemed to change to pleading, then to yearning. Then I noticed an intensity in his eyes. Perhaps it was understanding. Perhaps it was affirmation. I don't know. In a final gasp, he seemed to gather together all the scattered strands of his life. Then, in one last sigh, he breathed it all out—all his thirst, his dreams, his work, his fears. He seemed to let go of everything in that instant. In his dying I came to understand something about his living.

In that instant I knew that there is life after death. I came to this realization, not from any insight into a reality beyond the grave, but from the struggle that I experienced in this old man as he faced death. What I saw happening told me more about life than about death. The agony and the ecstasy of dying is an intensification of the struggle of life.

Birth and death, living and dying, are interrelated. We do not have to experience resurrection to believe this. We need only look prayerfully and with faith at the mystery of life. A Christian reverences every instant of life, but there are two moments that are especially sacred: birth and

death. Medically, we are gaining more control over
them. We are able to monitor birth and death, to
speed them up or slow them down. But, the mystery
still remains. There is something about them that is
beyond our ability to control. They are moments of
awe. They are experiences of gift.

The first thing we do when we are born is gasp for
breath. It is our first act of yearning. It is longing
for air. But it is more than that. It is a reaching out
for life. "I am thirsty," we seem to be saying. With
our whole being we yearn for life.

Life unfolds as a quest for fresh air. The pattern is
not just biological. It involves our total selves.
When we breathe in, we receive life. When we
breathe it out, it bears our own unique stamp. Just
as we transform the air we breathe, so we also
transform life as it flows through our inner selves.
The sensations and experiences of life emerge from
us as creativity and ideas, as poetry and conversation, as music and laughter. Life is the rhythm between our yearning to take in air and our desire to
breathe it out. Life moves between receptivity and
initiation, between contemplation and action, between receiving and sharing, between the yearning
to be filled and the longing to create fullness,
between grasping for the gift of life and letting it go.
This is the pattern of the journey we call life and
death. Its rhythm is found in every moment.

To understand this relationship between birth and death is to gain a key to the understanding of death as the fulfillment of life. For a Christian, death is not an absurd, cosmic accident that stops the process of life. It is our last creative act, the final breathing out of life. In death, we experience a coming together of life's rhythms. We have mistakenly called it the death struggle. It is really the *life* struggle. What began at birth as a great intaking of life is fulfilled at death in the final letting go.

Birth is like the first gasp for life, like March soil straining for warmth and air. Death is the harvest, the quiet stillness of a November night. Life is the struggle of April. In the opening words of *The Wasteland*, T. S. Eliot describes this mysterious struggle at the heart of life:

> "April is the cruellest month, breeding
> lilacs out of the dead land, mixing
> memory and desire, stirring
> dull roots with spring rain."[3]

Human life is an April journey toward fullness. The Marchs and Novembers of our lives are made present in the rhythm and the struggle of all our Aprils. We live between memory and desire, between breathing in and letting go, between "I thirst" and "it is finished." We are straining toward an experience that will transcend all our memories and desires. Each day we yearn to be filled with God.

Jesus is using more than a metaphor when he says that we must die to ourselves. He is speaking literally. First, I breathe in life. I open up to grasp it and change it. I take life to myself. I claim it as my own. But it is only fulfilled life to the extent that I let go of it. If I keep life to myself, it dies inside. On the other hand, if I die to myself, I release the gift of life. If I live with open hands, I come to fulfillment.

St. Paul believed that the death and resurrection of Jesus were not final events, but inward, daily experiences. He compares our lives to clay pots. God formed Adam out of clay and breathed life into him. So, too, he centers and shapes us with his love. We are only clay, but we carry within us the breath of God. We carry a treasure in our hearts, a mystery that leads to the fullness of life. "We are only the earthenware jars that hold this treasure to make it clear that such an overwhelming power comes from God and not from us. We are in diffi-culties on all sides but never cornered; we see no answer to our problems but never despair; we have been persecuted but never deserted; knocked down but never killed; always, wherever we may be, we carry with us in our body the death of Jesus so that the life of Jesus, too, may always be seen in our body. Indeed, while we are still alive, we are confined to our death every day for the sake of Jesus so that in our mortal flesh, the life of Jesus, too, may be openly shown" (II Cor 4:7-11).

The struggle between death and life in us is slow and quiet, but there are certain turning points. There are what Abraham Maslow refers to as "peak experiences." These are the times when the experience of life becomes intense and transparent. Peak experiences take place in the depth of our being. They cannot be put into words. They evoke our freedom and bring into focus all our feelings and energy.

Death is *the* peak experience of human life. It has ordinarily been understood as something external to us, an event that happens against our will. To a certain extent, this is true. We do not know nor can we control the circumstances of our death. But from the point of view of the gospel, death is not just an accident that happens to us. It is an inward event. It is a free experience. Viktor Frankl says that "everything can be taken from a man but one thing: The last of the human freedoms—to choose one's attitude in any given set of circumstances, to choose one's own way."[4] Death is our greatest act of decision. It is the last of the human freedoms. It cannot be taken from us because it is our breath, it is our life which is at stake. Only we can breathe it out.

The death of Jesus was, first of all, an inward experience that he faced and chose freely. "The Father loves me because I lay down my life in order to take it up again. No one takes it from me; I lay it down of my own free will and as it is in my power to lay it down, so it is in my power to take it up again; and this is the command I have been given by my Father" (Jn 10:17-18).

Each day we choose the way in which we take life in and breathe it out again. Each day we decide if we will die to ourselves and live for the gift of life. It is our inward stance of freedom which gives our lives their significance. The same is true of death. Death is our most significant act of inwardness and freedom. At that moment, we decide about our lives and their meaning, about how we breathe and share. Death is the coming together of all our feeling, reflecting and choosing. In the words of Ladislaus Boros, it is "the moment above all others for the awakening of consciousness, for freedom, for the encounter with God, for the final decision about our eternal destiny."[5]

Because death is the high point of our freedom, it is also the moment that we become most fully ourselves. Death is the realization of our personal destiny. While we are alive, we are not able to express ourselves fully. Our vision is only partial. We make faltering decisions and half-hearted commitments. We live on the surface. Human life moves in distraction and in fragmentation. Our dreams fall short, our decisions are weak and inconstant. In peak experiences, we come close to integration. But these are transitory, like something infinitely perfect seen in a passing glance.

God, who loves us as pilgrims, does not leave things unfinished. He accomplishes his word. He fulfills the experience of living. "I am quite certain," says St. Paul, "that the one who began this good work in you will see that it is finished when the day of Christ comes" (Ph 1:6). The Father brings the work of life and death to completion in each of us. He has already brought everything together in Jesus. Jesus responded to the Father so completely that the entire universe reaches fulfillment in him. St. Paul refers to Jesus as the *pleroma*—the fullness of God. The Father "brings everything together under Christ, as head, everything in the heavens and on the earth" (Ep 1:10).

When Jesus bowed his head and handed over the Spirit, he handed over his last breath. In that breath there is embodied the fullness of life. The breath of Jesus—the Spirit of Jesus—is the *Holy* Spirit. To die is to breathe one's last but, for Jesus, the last breath is the first breath of the new creation. The last breath of Jesus is the Spirit breathed into a new humanity. When we receive the Spirit, we receive the first glance of Jesus' new life. We receive the fulfillment of Jesus' life as the source of our own fullness.

It is in this sense that death is the fullness of life. It is in this sense that our daily dying becomes a way to fulfillment.

Ernest Hemingway's novel, *The Old Man and the Sea,* is a story about one person's struggle with life. In his combat with the sea, the old man symbolizes the struggle between death and resurrection that is part of every person's existence. The old man spent his life battling the sea—struggling with it. He also spent his life loving the sea—reaching out to it. Hemingway describes the old man with these words: "Everything about him was old except his eyes and they were the same color as the sea and were cheerful and undefeated."[6] In his life-struggle the old man had become physically weary. But inside he had grown young. His inner self had become one with the forces with which he struggled. His eyes were the color of the sea, the color of life. Even as his life moved toward November, his heart was filled with April.

As Christians we are invited to open ourselves to life, to plunge into it with all our energy, to cast out into the deep. We are called to discipleship. We are challenged to become vulnerable to the energy and power, to the terrifying force and creative promise that is human life. The gospel does not tell us that we will have an easy life. It does not remove suffering. It does not take away death. But it does offer a promise. It promises that if we live fully and deeply, we will begin to look like the sea. We will be filled with resurrection. Like the old man, our eyes will take on the color of life.

FOOTNOTES

1. Nikos Kazantzakis, *Zorba the Greek* (New York: Ballantine Books, 1965), p. 300.
2. Translation taken from Raymond E. Brown (Translator and editor), *The Gospel According to John,* Anchor Bible Series, 29a (New York: Doubleday, 1970), p. 898.
3. T. S. Eliot, "The Waste Land," in *The Complete Poems and Plays 1909-1950* (New York: Harcourt, Brace & World, Inc., 1952), p. 37.
4. Frankl, *Man's Search for Meaning,* 104.
5. Ladislaus Boros, *The Mystery of Death* (New York: Herder & Herder, 1965), p. IX.
6. Ernest Hemingway, *The Old Man and the Sea* (New York: Charles Scribner's Sons, 1952), p. 10.